Nikki Min Yeong Abramson

Choose I Hope

Overcoming
Challenges
with Faith
and Positivity

I Choose Hope
Overcoming Challenges with Faith and Positivity

Nikki Min Yeong Abramson

Forewords:

Tanya Baxter-BS, PT, PM &R Neurotoxin Clinic
Coordinator
University of Minnesota

Angela Thompson-Busch-MD, PhD
Pediatrician and Pediatric Clerkship Director

Rivershore Books

www.rivershorebooks.com

This edition: ISBN-13: 978-0615978512
ISBN-10: 0615978517
You may purchase the book through Rivershore Books or
Amazon.com, Barnesandnoble.com

Rivershore Books
www.rivershorebooks.com
info@rivershorebooks.com

Printed in the United States of America
www.renewingyourhope.com
www.nikkiabramson.com

Written by: Nikki Min Yeong Abramson
Book Cover Design: Scott Werley
Illustrator: Katherine Pjevach
Editors: Jansina and Gina Marinello-Sweeney (Rivershore
Books)
Editors: Brooke Vivian and Barb Wilson
Photo Credits: Kiera Johnson and Barb Wilson
Hair and Makeup Artist: Amber Walker
Author Headshot: Dani Werner

Acknowledgements and Thanks:

I write this book with a joy-filled heart in hopes that, through it, you may find encouragement, hope, and inspiration to press on in your own journey. There have been so many people that have helped me in my journey, and to each of you I want to say how much I appreciate your hard work. It truly takes a village, not only to raise a child, but also to write a book. Thank you to those of you who saw something in me and encouraged me to write my story. To every one of you who has been a part of my life journey: you have made a difference in my life and for that, I thank you.

First of all, to my Lord, Jesus Christ! Thank you for giving me a story to write and for being in every step of the way. Glory, honor, and praise goes to you, God!

Thanks to my wonderful, loving parents: Alan and Barb. You have been there for the ups and the downs, and I would not be who I am without you. Thanks,

Mom, for your helpful ideas and edits in making this book a true success. Thanks, Dad, for telling me "Nikki, you'll never write a book." This really encouraged me to write. Thanks to my brother, Anthony, for support in all I do. I love you, Bud, and am proud of you.

Thank you to all the amazing teachers, mentors, and leaders in my life. I appreciate all you do. Thanks to all the doctors and medical care teams that never gave up on me and saw me as a person and not a condition or disease. Thanks to all those that have been a part of my story, for allowing your stories to be in this book. I am grateful.

Huge thanks to those who have supported my writing: Tami Brown, Jenn Edwards, Jansina Grossman, Gina Marinello-Sweeney, Brooke Vivian, Kate St. Vincent Vogl, and Barb Wilson. Special thanks to my financial supporters through gofundme.com: Sun Mee Chomet, Holly Davis, Miguel Lindgren, Katie McElroy, and Scott Werley. Thank you to my parents for taking such great pictures of me growing up and allowing me to use them. To those that are in my writer's group and the Women of Words (WOW) for keeping me accountable and giving support and feedback. Special thanks to those who took the time to read my work and write reviews for my book. A huge hug and appreciation to my pediatrician, Dr. Angie Busch, and to Tanya Baxter, who plays a huge role in my care team, for writing forewords to my book. Please read them, as they give you a glimpse of two people in my life who have truly made a difference.

Editor and Publisher: Jansina and Gina Marinello-Sweeney (Rivershore Books)

Editors: Brooke Vivian and Barb Wilson

Book Cover Designer: Scott Werley

Illustrator: Katherine Pjevach

Pictures: Kiera Johnson and Barb Wilson
Hair and Makeup for Headshots: Amber Walker
Author Headshot: Dani Werner

Forewords

Tanya Baxter

This book is an enthusiastic celebration of the life of Nikki Min Yeong Abramson. I was introduced to Nikki when she arrived as a new patient in our Physical Medicine & Rehabilitation Clinic at the University of Minnesota Medical Center, Fairview, in the autumn of 2010. Nikki had been recently diagnosed with post-traumatic dystonia following a motor vehicle crash earlier that summer and was scheduled to be seen by the physician I work with, Dr. Dennis Dykstra.

I am Dr. Dykstra's care coordinator. The expertise I bring to this role is that I have been a registered physical therapist for over 40 years with an interest in neuromuscular and musculo-skeletal disorders. The partnership between Dr. Dykstra and myself originated in 1995 when we spent one half day clinic per week evaluating and treating patients with dystonia or spasticity with botulinum toxins. It sounds crazy I know, but the botulinum toxins help to normalize muscle tone in overactive or hypertonic muscles, thereby helping to provide improvement in motor control, comfort, and function. Almost twenty years later, we have nearly four full days per week of clinics treating patients with the botulinum toxins. Nikki is one of our patients.

Nikki's story is one of perseverance, bravery, and resilience. She is an amazing young woman who brings joy with her wherever she goes. She's also the most literal person I have ever met—hence the difficulty she has in determining whether Dr. Dykstra is teasing her or not. We've been working on her skills in that area for a couple of years now and I believe she's improving.

You will find Nikki's story fascinating and challenging. It is a unique tribute to the many hurdles she has faced with grace and aplomb, but even more, it is an example of profound resiliency in the face of often overwhelming challenges. When you need inspiration, just read a chapter of Nikki Min Yeong Abramson's I Choose Hope—you won't regret your choice.

Tanya Baxter, BS, PT,
PM&R Neurotoxin Clinic Coordinator

Angela Thompson-Busch

How can a medical disorder like mitochondrial myopathy cause such weakness in the muscles and body, yet such strength in the brain and soul of a person? Nikki Abramson is certainly the one that can answer that question. I have had the wonderful opportunity to know Nikki for over 15 years. I was privileged to be her pediatrician from the time she was the young girl on the cover of this book to the recent past.

Dressed in her gray school uniform, she would

come into the office and exude happiness with life. It never crossed my mind that she was making a conscious effort to be optimistic. I forgot that she was adopted—I simply forgot. She looked Asian, but she never appeared to have a hesitation with her self-confidence or identity. I wish I had asked her about her ethnicity, what her given name at birth was, if she wondered about her biologic family, or if she had any Korean personality characteristics. After reading this story, I realize that she made a conscious effort to remain optimistic through times of self-doubt. She chose hope.

I was the physician that told the blonde-highlighted teenage Nikki countless times to remember her epi-pen, go to sleep early, and take her medications faithfully. As she navigated through years of adolescence and young adulthood, she never suggested that having chronic illnesses, wearing a back brace, or taking a long list of medications was a nuisance. She never complained of her learning difficulties in school. I forgot that she had chronic illnesses—I simply forgot. She was involved in so many activities and so successful! It is no wonder that she was awarded such distinctions in high school. Instead of focusing on the difficulties in her life, she chose hope.

I was the physician that watched the exhausted Nikki try to fight countless viral illnesses while doing her student teaching. Her passion to teach was contagious, as were the many illnesses that her students shared with her in class. She would come in for difficulty breathing. I forgot that her muscles were weak, causing her to occasionally need a wheelchair. Often I saw her on a weekly basis and would ask her to take deep breaths. I forgot that she had muscle weakness, making every breath an effort—I simply forgot. She was determined to succeed in her chosen career and refused to let these little illnesses drag her down. She chose hope.

After Nikki's accident, I was also the one that optimistically (and often unrealistically) told Nikki week after painstaking week that her dystonia looked a lot better. I was the one that refused to give her steroids even though the medication made her feel stronger, scolded her for riding a motorized scooter without a helmet, and agreed to speak at her funeral if she died before me. I had no idea that she had been told as a child that with her disease she might die in her twenties. It never crossed my mind that when she was saying that "she was dying" in the office, she might have been thinking that she was really dying. I forgot that Nikki had fears—I simply forgot. She was inspirational and always chose hope.

One year ago, I told Nikki that I was changing my career path. I pride myself in providing medical care in a personal and humanistic way, so I had decided to move to a new community and work toward improving humanism in the graduate and post-graduate medical curriculum. Nikki's self-reflective story has humbled me. I realize that my superficial knowledge of Nikki and her medical condition did not give me any insight into the true person that she was. The faith, pain, and optimism that Nikki reveals throughout her story fills me with a strengthened resolve to try to learn more about a person, not just about their disease.

I felt that I knew almost everything about Nikki... until I read this book. Nikki mentions that adoption is a life-long journey. Her journey is an inspiring one thus far. I have gained so much insight into the feelings of a woman with chronic medical needs. For anyone who is working to find inner-strength, this book will help you find the way. For anyone who works in the medical field, or any person who is struggling to find hope, read this book. Nikki's resounding faith in God and herself is a true inspiration.

As a side note, I googled the word inspiration thinking it would help me get some ideas for writing this forward. Wikipedia had this quote: "Inspiration (from the Latin inspirare, meaning "to breathe into") refers to Nikki..." I do not understand what it means, but I agree.

Angela Thompson-Busch MD, PhD
Pediatrician and Pediatric Clerkship Director
Michigan State University College of Human
Medicine

Praise for "I Choose Hope"

This meaningful story really makes you think about your own. This strong, young woman encountered emotional and physical barriers that many people have not. It lets us know what it's like to truly be different. Before I read this, I thought that being adopted was just like being biologically related to your parents. Now I know that this is not true. This, her medical issues, and more help remind us that everyone is fighting a war. Some people just don't tell you. I'm glad she decided to tell us about hers.

Carmen Chavez, High School Student,
International School of MN

Nikki's story of perseverance is moving and inspiring. She takes us through her journey from childhood as a Korean adoptee, to her diagnosis of mitochondria and dystonia, to despair, and finally to a place of deep strength that can only be born from overcoming hardship. Faith is at the heart of Nikki's story and she communicates a beautiful gratitude towards all of the unsung heroes that have been a part of her journey: her parents, doctors, teachers, and friends.

It is tremendous to me that although Nikki has faced so many challenges, as a Korean adoptee and as a person handed so many unexpected physical challenges, her voice continues to resonate with momentous strength and a hope that is a lighthouse for all.

Nikki's story of perseverance is moving and inspiring. It is tremendous to me that, although she has faced so many challenges, as a Korean adoptee and as a person diagnosed with dystonia, Nikki's voice resonates with strength that is momentous and hope that we can all learn from. I am proud of her.

Sun Mee Chomet-Actor and Playwright of
How to be a Korean Woman and fellow
Korean adoptee friend

Nikki's story is about a young person's struggles with difficult life issues and the way she has managed to take the negatives and turn them into positives. I believe this book can help others who are in need of strength and encouragement to face their own life issues.

Dr. Dennis Dykstra,
Physical Medicine and Rehab MD, PhD.

I Choose Hope is an inspiring memoir of one Korean adoptee's life journey of hope, faith, and perseverance through adversity, shattered dreams, and racial identity. Sharing deeply personal experiences, Nikki invites the reader to walk alongside her as she recounts major life events, describes people who have made a significant impact in her life, and discovers her identity and life purpose. The book offers a raw look into the life of a person who has experienced many challenges but who has found hope, healing, and joy despite the pain—both physical and emotional—and disappointments. Readers will be amazed at the inner strength, determination, and unbreakable spirit of Nikki, a woman who has indeed chosen hope and continues to walk in faith and trust in the One who gives her grace to take each step.

Sarah Easton, adoption social worker

I've known Nikki for 8 years. She has been a great, encouraging friend, and her book is a true inspiration to me. I recommend reading her book, as it is a heartfelt account of overcoming obstacles in life. Titled *I Choose Hope*, this book imparts a feeling of hope and a sense of empowerment to accomplish anything that comes your way in life, despite fears and doubts. Reading *I Choose Hope* gives you strength to be the best you can be, no matter what, and provides a perspective and insight you can gain only by reading this book. It will make you feel more compassion, determination, and strength, within yourself as well as toward others. I highly recommend reading this book.

Being a Korean adoptee myself, I can identify with the experiences Nikki describes. As a Korean adoptee, with Korean features, but having inherited a very Scandinavian name from my adoptive parents, I am always amused at the surprised reaction of people that seem to have trouble accepting that a Korean born woman can have the name 'Johnson.' Although each adoptee's experience is different, we can all be enriched by and relate to the events Nikki describes as she chronicles her personal experiences with adoption and her unique struggles with disabilities. Though you may not realize she is living with disabilities by her appearance, this book will help you better understand Nikki's journey through life. I encourage you to read her book and learn more about what it's like to be adopted and to live with disabilities. I have been truly touched by reading it.

Brianna Johnson, an adoptee friend

In *I Choose Hope,* Nikki Abramson shares her journey through many unforeseen challenges and how she found encouragement and strength, not only to persevere, but to thrive. Leaning into her faith and the encouragement of mentors, parents, and teachers, Nikki has been able to grieve lost abilities and dreams, yet embraces the future with hope. This book not only recounts her journey, but gives tools to the reader to reflect upon their own lives and take healthy steps toward choosing a full and hope-filled life.

Deb Kielsmeier, Associate Pastor of Membership at
Christ Presbyterian Church

Nikki Min Yeong's *I Choose Hope* is an inspiration to teachers as she talks about the matching of the idea teachers have that they can change lives and serves as a reminder that in reality that actually does happen! Nikki knows and lives out the knowledge that we can do all things with strength from the Lord and that reliance on His saving grace and daily comfort allows us to live with energy and spunk!

Nikki is a naturally motivating person, and her personal story, reflection questions for us, and reference to quotes, people, and musicals is a powerful demonstration of hope, faith, perseverance, and positivity. This will be an inspiration to both students and teachers alike. It will encourage students as they deal with daily struggles to keep worries both big and small in perspective. Most definitely, it will fill teachers with a needed reminder that they truly do impact and influence student lives in positive ways! The title says it all—when Nikki tells her relevant story that although it is not always the easy decision to choose hope and positivity, doing so will bring joy to your life beyond what you could hope to happen!

Sarah Lindenberg,
High School Social Studies Teacher

As the title suggests, Nikki Abramson's *I Choose Hope* is a story of just that: hope. Regardless of the many challenges she has been dealt in her life, Ms. Abramson has managed to maintain a positive perspective and now uses her story to motivate others. Her journey through adoption and a complex cultural identity, in conjunction with several medical conditions, is an important reminder of our ability to persevere in the face of adversity. As a reader, one needn't share her same struggles to identify with the prevailing message that hope from within and help from others can provide a path to overcoming life's obstacles.

Jack Pipkin, Executive Director,
Muscular Dystrophy Association

There is a familiarity within *I Choose Hope* that makes it a very easy book to read. I attribute this to the tone in which the author tells her story. Despite addressing subjects that can be heavy, Nikki manages to find a way to explain things effortlessly, as if she were speaking about her experiences to a friend over a cup of coffee. However, what strikes me the most about the book is the abundance of positivity in the face of overwhelming adversity. Though she has already endured more obstacles than what many people will face in a lifetime, Nikki manages to exude strength and poise in all aspects of her life. Within the text, there are moments of reflection and grief, but at no point do things become uncomfortable. It is clear that Nikki has chosen to share many intimate details of her life, not for recognition or praise, but because doing so might help someone. In the world we live in, which is so often filled with negativity, it is nice to know that true stories of perseverance do exist.

Christy Scheid, Adoptee Friend

Nikki provides an excellent picture of what it is like to go through life with a disability. She paints a vivid portrayal of living with dystonia. Thank you, Nikki! Her book is a valuable guide for those going through challenges that push one's limits, as well as those supporting loved ones dealing with physical hardships. She shows us how to survive whatever life gives us through strength, faith, support, and most of all, hope.

Elizabeth Schultz, battles dystonia

Nikki, through her words, actions, and her book, *I Choose Hope*, shows us how a positive attitude, determination, faith, and HOPE can truly inspire us to overcome our obstacles and turn them into greatness and never-ending possibilities...

Kurt Seydow, battles dystonia

It has been quite some time since I picked up a book and got so riveted by it that I could not put it down. This book documents the challenges and trials that Nikki (the author) had to go through and how she faced her ordeal throughout her life to this day. If you are looking for a book that teaches you how to keep moving forward regardless of what your body is dictating to you, how to make "hope" the single focus of your life no matter what is being thrown your way, the importance of friendships in helping to keep your head above water and refocus your vision when all hope seem to vanish, and in making a triumph out of all the disasters that have piled up, look no more; this book is for you.

Nikki has an indomitable spirit that serves as a beacon of hope to all who know her or know her spirit. She has been an inspiration to many people throughout the world and is one of the best role models you can ask for. I have no doubt that her book will spread hope to all those who read it and I know she will be there egging them on every step of their personal journey.

I highly recommend this book.
Roger Soweid, SABIS® Corporate Director

Student Life and Student ManagementThe amount of difficulty that Nikki has endured and persevered through astounds me, especially since none of it is from any fault of her own, but from "the cards she was dealt": a relentless onslaught of physical disorders and disabilities that would make most people succumb, turn in their hand, and turn their back on life. However, listening to Nikki's story and knowing the person that she continually fights to be, it is incredibly clear to me that God has great things in store for her and is not done writing her story yet. I'm amazed to read her words: "I view my disabilities as my ability to help someone else;" those words should be an inspiration to all of us, since all of us deal with difficulties and inadequacies of our own. Those words should particularly bring hope to those who are walking down difficult paths that seem to have no end in sight. This book also gave me a renewed appreciation of all the people that have had a positive impact on my life who encouraged me to keep fighting and a renewed inspiration to bring hope and encouragement to everyone around me. You never know just how much saying "I believe in you" is going to mean to someone.
Laura Steen, college friend

.

Dedication

For all those that are overcoming, overcame, and will overcome. Never give up!

.

Table of Contents

"Struggles are a part of life. We can either go through it with a cloud over our head, or we can look at it as an opportunity."
- *Nikki Abramson*

Chapter 1:
Introduction: The Journey, Not the Destination

"Not to us Lord, not to us, but to Your name be the glory, because of Your love and faithfulness." - Psalm 115:1

I would not be here today without God, and for that I am grateful. This is a story of hope and a story of overcoming. It is a story of loss and a story of overcoming. It is a story of struggles and a story of overcoming. It is a story of ignorant comments and a story of overcoming. It is a story of identity and a story of overcoming. It is a story of hope—of choosing hope. I hope your minds and hearts are open to the idea and gift of hope, a gift we have the option of choosing every day.

So come, dive in with me, explore with me. I ask for your time, your devotion in reading my story, and some time in your own thoughts. Take a step. It is not easy. It may hurt along the way. However, I know that together we can do this.

I have always viewed writing as an activity that introverts enjoy. It is work you do as a single person (usually), not as a group of people. Being a 'people person', I didn't like the idea of working by myself. I would cringe at the thought of 'locking' myself in my room for days upon days to write, edit; edit, write. And…to do more writing and more editing. I viewed it as a 'waste of time.' I'd much rather spend time with people and share my story over a cup of coffee.

When I write a piece, I tend to write it, edit it, rework a few things, and be done. I'm an extrovert, type A, achiever, and a 'get it done and move on to the next project' person. After a few years of Caribou Coffee dates with my laptop and my decaf skim vanilla latte, I disciplined myself to complete the task at hand. As an extrovert, I am certainly glad that this part of my writing is done.

I had many aspirations and dreams growing up. I wanted to be a youth pastor, an event planner, a performer, a politician, and an elementary school teacher. I hoped to one day become a school principal. I knew my calling was to work with people. I felt called to teach when I was in the third grade and never looked back since. In fact, I completed degrees in elementary education, early childhood education, and computer technology education. But one thing I never aspired to was to write a book. I never thought that I'd write one. It was not on my 'to do' list or 'bucket' list. Although I enjoy writing and much prefer writing a paper to objective tests, I would not consider myself a writer, let alone an author.

I have many job titles. If you call my voicemail, you hear: "Hi, you have reached Nikki Abramson; teacher, coach, mentor, performer, teaching artist, motivational speaker, and educator..." Writer is not in that message. In spite of this, I chose to begin this book. My intention is to inspire, to guide, to encourage, and to motivate you. I am not here to say that I have it all together; in fact, I am far from that. I am not here to say my life is so hard or my life is so amazing. I have come to the point, though, that I can say I am blessed and thankful to be alive and share a piece of my journey with you. My story and journey led me to live a life that is hopeful, inspiring, and positive.

If I am not a writer, then why write, you might ask. Writing came out of the encouragement from friends. People in my life said I had a powerful story—why not share it with the world? I can't even begin to tell you how many people ask, "How do you stay so positive? You have such a joyful spirit and energy. How do you do it? I really admire your strength to keep going despite the challenges you endure. You really need to tell your story." I know that even through the hardest of times, I still hold strong. What is the secret to this hopefulness? Realize that the best is yet to come. Realize that you have potential. Realize that you have *many* gifts to offer this world. Realize that God is not finished with you yet. Realize that there are *so* many blessings in your life. We can't take life for granted.

Why write a book when you are such an extrovert? I don't know, but I began to realize that writing my story was a calling: my mission, my destiny, and my dream. I hope that this story/God's story will fill your soul.

As I mentioned, I am not a writer (although I'm trying to embrace this new title in my life).However, I credit Jenn Edwards, my high school English teacher, as the person who instilled a passion and desire to write. Without this passion, I would not be able to sit at Caribou Coffee for the hours upon hours needed to write this book. It all started in ninth grade English class. I remember it as if it was yesterday, but it was 2001 to be exact.

Every week, Mrs. Edwards would ask us to write a journal entry to practice writing. She gave us a topic, and for fifteen minutes we had to write. No questions, no talking, just writing. At first, I finished writing on the topic in about five minutes, said I was done, and sat there until we moved on. Gradually, after a few months, I found my 'voice' and wanted to keep writing longer than our allotted fifteen minutes. The writing prompts were inspiring.

After we wrote, Mrs. Edwards collected our work and gave us feedback if we desired. I loved her feedback, as it was helpful and critical. It pushed me on more. I still have those journal entries and re-read them once in a while to remind myself of how I came to where I am today.

Mrs. Edwards found something in my writing and helped me to develop this skill and find my 'voice.' I am so grateful for her interest in my fifteen-year-old self and for taking me under her wing. Jenn and I are great friends today; in fact, I am beyond grateful for the fact that she has helped encourage me all throughout high school, college, and my adult life. She even allowed me to stay at her house in California to write. I am thankful for having an editor that knows me, my story, my writing style, and my voice so well.

At the end of the school year, we were asked to write a personal narrative about ourselves—specifically, a topic we had to overcome. I loved that term; as I reflect upon it, overcoming has been a theme in my life. I wrote about having mitochondria myopathy, a disability I was born with, and how it impacted my life. This essay taught me how to express what I had overcome. It also made me realize that I am thankful for the challenges I have had, as they have made me who I am. My thoughts evolved from a ninth grade term paper to this book.

"These problems have brought me closer to my friends and to God. This year, I have seen God work in mysterious ways through this condition and I will always remember the verse, "I can do all things through Christ who gives me strength." Philippians 4:13" (Except from overcoming 9th grade paper)

One of my all-time favorite movies is *Sister Act Two*. It is an entertaining, inspiring musical with a good message. Whoopi Goldberg's character, Sister Mary Clarence, encourages people that you truly can change the world. In the movie, she teaches a group of inner city high school students: "If you want to be somebody, if you want to go somewhere, you better wake up and pay attention." Wake up! I've learned to wake up, and I hope you do as well. She changed her students' worlds, and you can change yours. My motto in life has become "You can change the world." I truly believe in the power of hope to bring about change. If you have hope and faith in someone, you can make a difference. This is what the world needs more of. If you haven't seen this movie, check it out; it changed my thought process and the way I viewed life.

Often people come into our lives for a reason. You will find in this book many people that have truly come into my life for a reason. These people are leaders, teachers, doctors, care teams, friends, youth leaders, but ultimately mentors. In need of inspiration, I turn to the words of the song "For Good" from the Broadway hit musical *Wicked*. Check it out if you don't know it. It is an amazing song. I am who I am today because of the many mentors, teachers, leaders, and friends in my life. I thank each of you for what you've given me, and I am forever grateful for your inspiration, friendship, mentorship, and dedication to seeing me grow. It truly does take a village to raise a child.

I've written this book to fill you with stories of my life. Some of the stories may make you laugh or smile, whereas others may bring tears to your eyes. The stories in this book are simply about overcoming—overcoming challenges, yet seeing the positive, the good, and the hope in them. It is my desire that these stories will not be just stories, but something you can hold on to when there is little to no light at the end of the road. We have so much to be thankful for, yet we don't often stop to even think about or appreciate it. Over the last several years, I have been given that time. Whether or not I used it well, I don't know, but I urge you to reflect on your own story and know how valuable it is, how valuable you are, how much you contribute to this society, and how you make a difference in others' lives. Remember: it is the journey, not the destination.

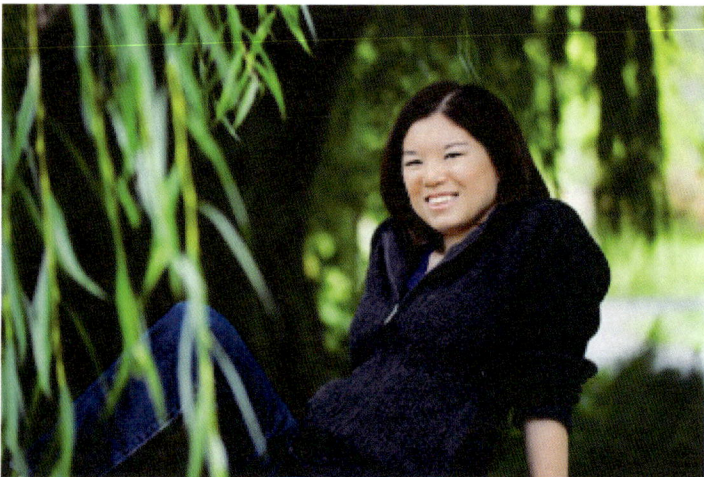

Writing has become a way for me to express my deeply-felt need to get this message out—this message of hope. I am writing for the girl who struggled in school, for the boy with severe medical challenges, for the family who lost their loved one, for the twenty-year-old trying to find their way in the world, for the forty-year-old that lost his job, for the one who is overcoming...I am writing for you.

We all encounter challenges, whether we like them or not. I believe we should grow and learn from them. It is about how we choose to live and our perspective in life. Do you see the glass half full or half empty? Are you living in the present or looking at the past? As you read this book, I encourage you to ask yourself:

1.   Do I take life for granted? What can I do to appreciate every minute?
2.   What are the battles that I am struggling with?
3.   How can I overcome them?
4.   What can I do to choose hope?
5.   What does hope mean? What does it look like to me?

Maybe that means going to Barnes and Noble, buying a journal and a cup of coffee, and writing. Reflect upon your blessings. What are you called to do? Take a risk? Think outside the box? Maybe it is to just sit back, relax, and enjoy the ride.

The cover of the book represents a young girl looking out into her future. This young girl is me. The picture was taken when I was about five or six years old. My mom tells me the story of wanting to dress myself, hence the miscellaneous early 90s look: one knee-high sock up, vest, kid bracelet, and blanket in arm. My shirt says "survival gear." I was standing on the stairs outside of our house, getting ready to go to an event. My mom took the picture. She says that for her, it captures her little girl's courage looking towards the future. The background behind me represents the sun and light in the distance, depicting hope. The mountains and hills represent the journey and struggles I've climbed. Thanks to Scott Werley for incorporating these ideas into a single picture.

Many people ask me about the title, *I Choose Hope*, and how that came to be. Honestly, I feel like I was hit with it in a dream; not in a weird way, but in a "God" way. It has been on my heart since sinking my teeth further into telling this story. Here's the deal: we all have choices we need to make throughout our days and our lives. Choices of what drink to order at our local coffee shop. Choices about whether we go to this college or that university. Choices about whether we take this job or that job; marry this person or not. Choices can be life-changing ones or small ones. Both are a choice. I believe that we need to choose hope. This is not a one-time choice, but a choice that we need to make over and over again. I have chosen hope and try to live out a life that is hopeful. I have learned to choose hope. It was a battle in many ways with the obstacles I've overcome, but I have learned to live in the present and choose hope through faith and positivity.

This book is divided into sections based on several significant challenges in my life and the overcoming hope that I have experienced through them. The beginning of each chapter includes each a verse or a song title that relates to the chapter. At the end of my story, there are a few chapters of hope and inspiration. I leave you with some journal questions for you to think about, and journal on, as well as a list of resources that have inspired me throughout my life. You will also find many pages at the back of the book that are reflections of my journey through dystonia (a medical condition) at the website www.caringbridge. org. I wanted to include them for you to journey with me through some of my hardest times. I want to thank Caring Bridge for being a place where I can share my thoughts, feelings, and let others know what I am going through.

If I can impact the life of one person, my job is done. While I am not teaching an academic subject like I thought I'd be doing, had studied to do, and poured my life into doing, I hope to use my teaching skills to share my thoughts on the ideas of overcoming, hope, motivation, inspiration, dedication, and love.

Sometimes the road is bumpy, and other times it is smooth sailing. Like in *The Wizard of Oz,* I have followed a 'yellow brick road.' This road may have curved a bit, but it was clear and evident where you go next. There were other times where the road was long, windy, and curvy, with little light showing which direction to go, like the ride Space Mountain at Disney World. You have no idea where you are going, as there is little to no light shining the direction the ride will go. Both roads have given me a perspective of life that I have learned and gleaned from, making me the strong person I am today.

My hope is that this book will inspire you and guide you down your own road. Open your heart and open your mind, so that we can truly journey on this road together.

Are you ready? Before you jump in with me, do me a favor. Close your eyes. Imagine you had ten more years to live. Just ten. Think about that for a minute. Now, think as though you were six years old and you are told you had ten more years to live. Just ten. What are your thoughts? How will you live? Now add on to this ten years; imagine yourself with an unknown medical history with little information about your birth family. What types of struggles will you encounter? Okay, now that you have this picture in your mind, let's go!

Chapter 2:
Friday, August 29, 1986

*"For I know the plans I have for you declares the Lord,
plans to prosper you and not to harm you, plans to
give you a hope and a future." - Jeremiah 29:11*

They say that those who fight are those that win the battle. If I ever wanted a reason to fail, I had plenty. Too many times, it seemed like I could not succeed. Too many times, I thought failure and giving up was easier. I had plenty of reasons to lose hope, to think that Jesus didn't believe in me. It takes true courage, though, to fight. Those that fight truly win.

Names give us an identity—a special identity. In order to connect with someone, you need to know their name. This is what you will be called for the rest of your life. Many parents spend hours upon hours tossing around different names. These names could be family names, Biblical names, or just names that sound pleasant. There is often a story for naming a child or a reason behind that name. I believe names give value, identity, and significance.

My name is Park, Min Yeong. Min Yeong means 'bright, shining, and good natured.' I was born in Kyonggi-Do, a province outside Seoul, South Korea. I was adopted at the age of six months.

박 민영-Park, Min Yeong

I was born on Friday, August 29, 1986, weighing a mere six pounds. I can only imagine what it was like on that day. Many people know the exact time they were born, their weight, how long they were, the location of their birth, and their parents' names. They probably have pictures of themselves minutes after their birth or perhaps even a video recording of being placed into their mother's arms. Most have pictures of their parents in the hospital with their baby, the baby gazing into the mother's eyes while the mother gazes back. They may have beautiful pictures, videos, and memories of the parents bringing the baby home from the hospital and settling into a new environment. The mom's tears of joy when the baby first cries, the father's look at the mother in amazement of what they created together, the mother exhausted, yet in utter awe.

I don't have any of that. Instead, I came on an airplane with a mini pink album consisting of ten pictures that were taken of me with the foster care family that I lived with before coming to Minneapolis, Minnesota. Some are pictures that I'll cherish forever, just getting a small glimpse into what my life was like before coming to America.

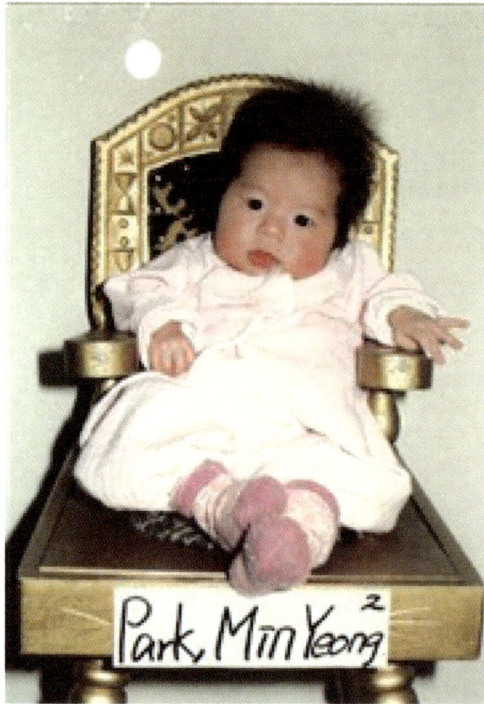

Park, Min Yeong

What I have is a record—a file that the agency provided my parents—with everything from medical history and family life to a few pictures. According to the file, I endured failure to thrive. This was challenge number one in my life. Failure to thrive in infants means that they aren't able to take in, retain, and utilize calories needed to gain weight and grow. I was not gaining enough weight to survive. It was as though I was taken away from my birth mother and said, "No. I can't do it," and struggled to exist. I can only begin to imagine what it would have felt like to struggle to survive.

Would I live? I imagine that as a newborn, my soul had lost hope. Yet I somehow managed to fight on. There was something inside of me saying not to give up; to keep going and keep running the race. God was not finished with me yet!

According to my Korean medical records, I started to show improvement on December 2, 1986. I started to gain weight and began thriving. Overcoming!

There was hope. Because of this, there are times I celebrate my birthday twice: my official birthday, August 29th, and the birthday of December 2nd, the date my records show my soul started to live again and my body started to gain weight. Developmentally, I was three months behind my birthdate.

The failure to thrive slowed my adoption out of Seoul to experience my new soul and identity as a Minnesotan. On February 7, 1987, I made a long journey (24 hours) to the Minneapolis/St. Paul airport with several other babies and a social worker from Seoul.

This began my new life and a new chapter in my book: a chapter that involved leaving my Korean heritage and the first five and half months of my life as a Korean to become an American. A chapter of which I have neither memories nor understanding.

After a very long flight, I arrived to loving parents and friends anxiously awaiting my arrival. There were many people there surrounding me with cards, balloons, cameras, toys, and love. The social worker gave me to my new 'Mom and Dad.' I imagine how bewildered and confused I must have been, getting off a taxing flight and being put into the arms of complete strangers who kept saying how much they loved me and had been thrilled for my arrival. People wanted to hold me and said how cute I was. My parents were as tired as I was, waiting and preparing for me for years. I was tired, due to the drastic time zone changes. After the initial excitement, we left the airport for my new home. Excited as my parents were, I was confused about everything that was going on. Attaching to my birth mother, attaching to my foster care family, and then to my parents—this was the beginning of an exciting adventure!

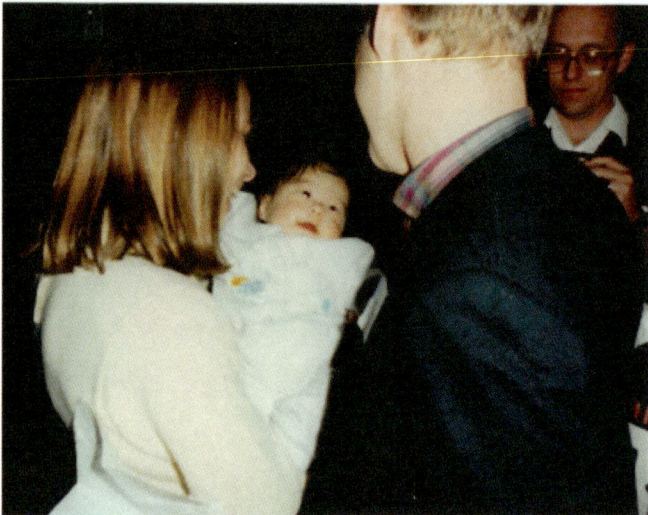

Chapter 3:
Who am I?

"I don't think we are in South Korea anymore."
- Nikki Abramson

When I arrived in Minnesota, I was given a new name, and it became my new identity. After carefully considering several of names from the list that my parents' friend made for them, ranging from Emily to Lauren, my parents gave me the name Nikki. After all, they loved the *Nick at Night TV show* and the Nike shoe brand. Nikki means victory to the people, victorious. My parents chose to keep my given name, Min Yeong, as my middle name, to honor my Korean heritage. Today, I carry the name Nikki Min Yeong to recognize both my Korean and American cultures. I love my name, as it truly embodies who I am: a 'bright, shining, good-natured, and victorious one.'

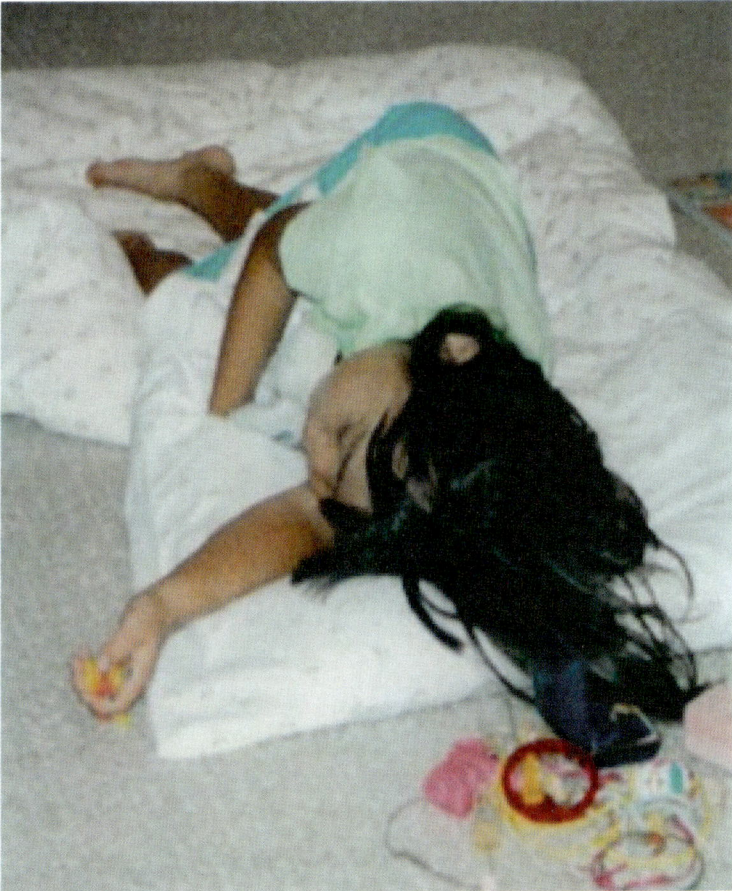

There were many cultural adjustments I had to make with my new 'home.' As a six month old, I had to learn to relinquish my Korean culture and way of life and learn to become American. Several months after arriving, I became a U.S. citizen. I could tell that even as an infant, the U.S. was different.

In Korea, families sleep on the floor together. The crib was a place to play. My American parents apparently didn't get the memo. Cognitively, I felt something was strange about America. People didn't sleep on floors, and when I was put in the crib that meant sleep time. I have a very vivid memory of my first several months, which revolves around a book. It was a picture book, full of pictures of Korea and the Korean culture. As I went through this book as a toddler, I would keep flipping to this one page. This page showed a family that *all slept together on mattresses on the floor.* I would show my parents this page every time they put me to sleep. I thought that was the way it was supposed to be: everyone on the floor together. My infant self didn't understand that we don't do that here in America. Regardless of the time zone difference, I thought that when I was in my crib it was time for me to play and when I was on the floor, it was time for me to sleep. Something in me still loves sleeping on the floor and in close proximity to others. I guess I hold that part of my Korean heritage.

Another challenge I went through as a child was the fact that my parents didn't look like me nor did the other faces I saw for the second six months of my life. When I first came off the plane and was handed to my parents, I poked their eyes and noses and flipped their hair as if there was something wrong with them. Why

didn't they look like the people I grew up with? Where were their Korean facial features? No black hair? As a mere infant, I struggled to know who I was and where I was. I was taken away from my birth mother, a mother whose calm voice I would listen to in the womb and whose dark brown eyes and hair I would look for as an infant.. I was taken away from her and put into foster care. In foster care, I lived with a family who showered me with love, yet I was listening for that familiar sound. As soon as I got used to these people, I was brought to America, where I would adjust to a new set of eyes, faces, sights, and sounds. When I had arrived at the place I now call 'home', it took me months to adjust to this new culture, new way of life, new time zone, and new way of doing things. There was something in my soul that was left in Seoul, telling me not to give up. This became a recurring theme for me: 'never give up; overcome your challenges.'

Being Korean and American has caused me much confusion. Am I Korean or am I Caucasian? Which box do I check when asked for my ethnicity? How do I respond to someone asking me where I am from? How do I identify myself? At various points in my life, I felt conflicted. Do I say that I am American, when that is what I feel? I feel 'white.' Or do I say Korean when I really don't feel Korean? Even though on the outside I look one way, I feel another. How do I embrace both cultures? At times, I felt I didn't fit in with either the American or Korean culture. It is as though I am half one thing and half another, like biracial kids having one culture and another culture that come together. I felt as though I could relate to missionary kids. They look American, yet they grow up with a different upcoming life experience, which in a way is similar to mine. Being adopted is its own separate category in which many, yet few at the same time, can relate to. It is as though adoptees have their own category, their own language, their own group.

I always remember celebrating a few special days a year besides holidays. Those days were: my birthday (August 29), when I started to come out of failure to thrive (December 2), and my Gotcha Day (February 8). In fact, my brother, who is seven years younger than I am (also adopted, but from Paraguay), has the same Gotcha Day as I do. What a fun and unplanned day for my parents!

I am sure that some of you reading this are saying to yourself what is "Gotcha Day"? Gotcha Day is the day that you arrived to your parents and became theirs. It is the day you come to America. Some people call it 'airplane day.' My family celebrates it every year. When I was younger, my parents gave us small gifts. Today, we celebrate the day by going out for dinner together. Gotcha Day is almost as big as your birthday, as this is the day you arrived to your new family.

There are other Korean traditions my family celebrates. On New Year's Day in Korea, children dress up in formal wear called *hanboks*. Children bow to their elders to show respect. They receive money and gifts in exchange. For many years on New Year's Day, I did the same: dressed up in my hanbok, bowed to my parents, and got money. My American Girl doll even dressed up as well. We occasionally celebrate Children's Day.

Children's Day is a national Korean holiday similar to Mother's Day or Father's Day, in which children are celebrated. It occurs in early May and often my family took me to see a theatre show or concert for it. Doing these cultural activities instilled some sense of purpose and identity in being a Korean American. I think they formed who I am and helped me feel pride in who I am.

Since there are so many Korean adoptees in the Twin Cities area, there was a camp that I attended for many years. Every summer, from first grade to eighth grade, I attended Korean Culture Camp. Korean Culture Camp (KCC) was such a fun and enriching camp where I learned more about who I am and my heritage. I always thought it was interesting to learn some of the Korean Hangul language, culture, tae kwon do, cooking, and art classes. I learned to count to five in Korean, say hello and thank you, and sing the Korean National Anthem. I thought it was inspiring, as many people there looked like me. For one week, I was surrounded with people that 'got it,' who understood, and who looked like me. In this week-long camp, we formed this unspoken connection of being Korean adoptees. It was like we knew we would always be friends, no matter what. It gave us an identity that we truly embodied. It was the one place I didn't look different, and we all knew what the other was going through. Today many of my friends are still from Korean Culture Camp. I also try to volunteer with the camp when I am able. It truly made a difference in my life knowing there are other people that had similar life experiences as I did.

There were many social events put on through Children's Home Society agency that I also participated in. Honestly, I usually didn't want to go to these events. I wanted to be like my other American friends. Even though there would be many adoptees there, I didn't necessarily want to attend. At these gatherings, there would be a Korean dinner and some sort of entertainment like Korean drumming, dance, or tae kwon do (karate). There would be many vendors trying to sell you a bunch of Korean stuff. Every time, my mom asked me if I wanted something that represented Korea. I looked around the ornate table displays and said "no," thinking to myself, *This doesn't represent my culture.* My culture is American, in Minnesota, not in South Korea. Despite me telling my mom "no," she bought me something every time anyway. To this day, I have a huge drawer full of Korean things ranging from Korean children's books both all in Korean and half Korean/English, magazines, books on tape, language on tape, dolls, flags, clothes, and picture books. This was another way for me to overcome a challenge of adjustment and provided me with hope.

Every so often, in high school, when I was going through things in my room to get rid of or sell, I would say, "I would like to sell my Korean stuff," but my mom made me keep it. She said I would enjoy it when I got older. As I matured, I discovered this drawer is a sacred drawer for me. It means memories, understanding, and awareness, and is symbolic for me that my culture is not only American, but also Korean. For this, I am thankful.

My parents asked me at various stages of life if I had any interest in going to visit Korea. I glanced at the brochure and quickly said "no." My culture is here. My home is here. I am American. Why would I want to go to visit Korea? I felt as though people would look at me and wonder why I wouldn't speak Korean. However, as an adult, I now feel that visiting Korea will allow me to know what it is like and experience what my life might have been. Someday, I hope to go back to Korea. No matter how hard I fight being Korean, I realize that there are several inherent traits that are innate in me from my Korean culture.

Here are just a couple of things that I feel are innate Korean aspects about me:

1.   I love spicy food! Always have and always will. I always add a lot of spice to my food and people look at me as if I am crazy. You will burn your

mouth out, people tell me, however the spicier the food the better.

2. Koreans love martial arts. They, in fact, started tae kwon do. This is very similar to karate. Without knowing this or having any prodding from anyone, I asked my mom if I could sign up for karate at the age of six. I competed with National Karate for years and received my brown belt.

3. Many Koreans enjoy the guitar. This is one of my first instruments I learned to play and the only one chosen entirely by myself, rather than my parents. I fell in love with the guitar. I enjoyed playing ever since and still play to this day.

4. Gift giving is huge in Korea. People who know me well know I love giving gifts and am a pretty talented gift giver. I know what people like and what to give people. Giving gifts makes me so happy.

5. Family and paying respect to your family is very important in Korea and to me. I will drop everything for my family and friends. They are the most important thing, other than God, in my life.

6. Hard work is another huge value for Koreans. I value hard work and am always considered a hard-working person. I always give 110% to whatever I do.

7. If you know me well, you will know that I enjoy asking questions, especially personal questions. Koreans also ask a lot of questions, especially personal ones. When grabbing coffee with me, be prepared for a plethora of them.

8. I study a lot and actually enjoy studying. I take it seriously. Koreans do as well.

9. Koreans love festivals and celebrating holidays. I am all about festivals, holidays, celebrations, parties—you name it. I go 'all out' for every holiday. Any time I get to celebrate, I love it!

10. I love sleeping on the floor. I much prefer to sleep on the floor on a mattress or sleeping bag rather than on a bed. I also love it when people sleep in the same room. This is what it is like in Korea as well. When I was a child, I voluntarily asked to sleep in a sleeping bag on our porch's patio.

11. Norebong is huge in Korea. Norebong is basi-

cally the Korean version of karaoke. I love singing and karaoke. I had no idea that this was so huge in Korean culture.

Names are important. Being called Park, Min Yeong is so different. It is something I didn't want. I wished I could embrace my Korean name, yet never felt it was a part of me. Through my journey, I am learning to embrace my name, Nikki Min Yeong: the bright, shining, good-natured, and victorious one.

Chapter 4:
Korean or American?

"You Can't Stop the Beat" – Hairspray

How you identify yourself is a crucial part in your journey. I thought to myself, am I Caucasian or am I Asian? What box do I check on surveys when they ask for my race? How do I respond to the question "Where are you from?"

How does this cultural identity play a role into the idea of overcoming and hope? Well, I needed hope. I needed to feel like I had a purpose as a Korean American. I needed to overcome an obstacle of people's stubbornness, ignorance, prejudice, misunderstanding, and lack of knowledge. This was a challenge. I think many people don't realize how challenging it can be to look one way but really be something else. I taught preschool Spanish for a year, and to be honest, it was a little weird for me. Even though I loved the job, here these preschool kids are seeing an Asian face, perhaps thinking I will speak or even know some Asian language, and what comes out of my mouth is not Korean but Spanish! Many times, I didn't want much of anything to do with my Korean culture, as I wanted to 'fit in.' Because I knew much more of the Spanish language and Hispanic culture, I often related more with the Latinos than the Asians. I wanted to be a person that looked like others rather than have people guessing about my background. It got so tiring, having to explain all the time who I was and where I was from.

Ever since I was a young child, I realized that the color of my skin didn't match my parents and my hair was black and straight, not like theirs. I always wondered how I got my creative side or my determination. Did I inherit any characteristics of my birth parents?

Despite the curiosity, I am consumed with the weird stares that people give me when I am out and about. It is as though they think to themselves "Where did you come from?" I call it 'the look.' I get this 'look' all the time: going to the mall with friends, eating out, going to shows, and at school; you name it. I got 'the look' from future dorm mates who were excited to meet me freshmen year in college. Judging by my last name, Abramson, they thought I would be a typical blue-eyed, blonde-haired girl from Bloomington. So, when we met at school, I got 'the look' because I wasn't who they thought. They looked as though they didn't understand me, as though they didn't know who I was. Sometimes people would even speak extra slowly to me, so I would understand what they were saying. They could not see past the fact my facial features were that of Asian descent. The 'look' follows me wherever I go. People make assumptions about me; they assume that I am from someplace else. Initially, it is silly, yet it also tears me to the core. I am from South Korea, which is my heritage, my background, where everything started. Yet I have an American culture, background, upbringing, and life-experience.

Another story of ignorance and lack of understanding came from my college years. A friend suggested that we go to get Chinese food. She thought I was Chinese.

1. I am not Chinese.
2. I don't enjoy Asian food.

I prefer Tex-mex Mexican or Italian food. Why can't more people understand? I am adopted. I don't feel Korean, yet I don't fit in with the American culture. While I felt different enough with my medical conditions (which I will explain later), I felt even more different because I didn't look like most of the students at school—or, for that matter, the people in my community.

I went to Bethel University in St. Paul, Minnesota for my undergraduate degree. Bethel was a wonderful school, and I received an excellent education there. However, Bethel challenged me racially. When I got accepted to Bethel and checked a box that I was Asian, I got assigned a certain admissions counselor that works with students of color. I was invited to a freshmen orientation specifically for students of color where you move in early, meet people, and get acquainted with the Bethel community. I almost threw the invitation letter away. My parents convinced me to go, as it would be a good idea to move in early and meet people in a smaller group setting. After much bartering, I agreed to attend the special orientation. I can't even begin to thank my parents for 'making me' go; some of the people I met those first few days ended up being my roommates for three years and are some of my closest friends today. We had the most diversity of any dorm room, with people from all over the world. While I remember our room standing out at Bethel, it reminded me of my 'ISM home' (my high school), which was such a richly-diverse school.

At Bethel, I thought I was like everyone else. I had the same upbringing as most students, but I was put into the box of students of color. As a member of that box, people expected me to have a very different life experience. I was pushed towards leading activities and clubs for students of color. As a leader, I did it. I loved it—the students, my team, my experiences—and it became a passion, yet my heart was in what the mainstream students were doing.

My time at Bethel led me to become an intern for the Office of Student Life: Intercultural Student Programs and Services. I led a student mentor program as well as the freshmen orientation program; the program I resisted to go to. While I was a leader there, my supervisor, Terrence Galbreath, instilled hope in me. He was put in my life for a reason. Terrence and I worked together to put a mentor program in place as well as developed a freshmen orientation for students of color. Terrence and I worked well together on a leadership basis, and he helped me to see who I am. He was a mentor to me in leadership and in school, and he still is. I am grateful for Terrence for teaching me more about culture and helping me to embrace mine. When I felt different from the student body, I knew that I could always come to him for anything. We all need more mentors like that.

Throughout preschool, elementary, middle, high school, college, and now as an adult, people made fun of me or said ignorant comments to me about my race. Although I have many friends who see me and not my race, there were people made fun of my squinty eyes and my Asian-looking nose. I always had small facial features, and it was hard for my parents to buy me shoes as I had the smallest and narrowest feet. I still do. It never really bothered me, but I wanted to 'fit in' and be like others. *How come no one looks like me?* I wondered as I looked around the room at my school. I stood out in the crowd. I looked 'different' but felt like everyone else. I am yellow. I am like a banana or an Oreo cookie, dark on the outside and white on the inside. Actually, the heart of interracial adoptee experience reflects this type of analogy. Most of us adoptees are able to understand this analogy.

Here I am, trying to live my life, and I get questions about who I am. These have caused me to question my identity. Here are some of the most common struggles that I have experienced as an adoptee (although there are many more not listed here). Also, note that this is my experience and not every interracial international adoptee feels this way:

1.   When you tell someone your last name is Abramson and they expect you to look like a Swedish-European rather than a Korean. They expect one thing and you turn out to be another. It is always interesting to meet someone that I have never met before and they try to look for me, thinking I am something I am not.

2.   People start speaking to you in another Asian language. I have no idea what they are saying to me. No, I don't speak Korean or Chinese or Japanese.

3.   People assume I am similar to my parents both in personality and in looks. No, I don't look like anyone in my family.

4.   Is there a chance of cancer in your family? How about diabetes or MS? Am I more likely to get a disease? I have no idea! I don't know my medical history. It is unknown.

5.   Where are you from? I'm from Bloomington. No, really, where are you from? Bloomington. Oh, you mean my ethnicity or where I was born. I'm Kore-

an. This is a very common conversation for me.

6.   Americans think I'm married and changed my last name. Koreans think I am so old to not be married yet.

7.   You must be really good at math. Many Asians, especially Koreans, are. No, I am not really good at math. In fact, I failed my sophomore year math class.

8.   What does it feel like to be adopted? Well, what does it feel like to not be adopted? It's hard to say if something is your only experience. What are some of the challenges you have had as an adoptee? I can't speak for all Korean adoptees, or even adoptees. I only have my own experience as an international-interracial, Korean American adoptee.

9.   What languages do you know? English and Spanish. No, what other languages do you know? Uh, just English and Spanish...and a few words in French, Dutch, and Korean.

10. Who are your real parents? What does that mean, real parents? My parents are my parents. I don't have real or fake parents.

11. When I tell people that I am from Korea, they ask me, "Are you from North or South," just to make sure with all that is going on with North Korea.

12. Can you teach me something about your culture? What exactly do you want me to tell you?

Middle school years are formative years in a person's life. Everyone wants to be 'normal' and be like others. I wanted to be 'white' like many of my friends, not 'yellow.' I asked my parents if it would be okay to highlight my hair blonde. In seventh grade, my parents agreed to let me highlight it. I remember going to the hair salon, thinking I was going to have blonde highlights and look 'more normal.' My hair went from dark brown to blonde highlights. After many years of highlights, my hair was almost entirely blond. I loved it! I had hoped that I would fit in and appear more like others. In college, I wanted to go back to dark brown hair and dyed it all back to dark brown/black hair. Going back and forth in my hair colors defined my identity and who I was. I thought that a certain color hair would make me more Caucasian. To this day, I still highlight my hair, because I like how it looks, not because of how I think others view me. The highlights now are copper, not blond.

People don't understand why I have a Swedish last name and look Asian. When I call someone on the phone to make an appointment, they expect someone else because of my last name. When I was looking at colleges, a current student at the school asked me where I was from. I said "Bloomington." They said,

"No, where are you from?" I kept saying, "Blooming-ton," as if they didn't understand me. I was confused by their question. We danced around this question for a few minutes. They even began speaking slower as if I were from another country and not understanding their question. Finally, I gave up and said I was born in South Korea and I was adopted. I still get this question. Ah, the frustrations of being an international, inter-racial adoptee.

People also ask, "So, how long have you lived here? You speak good English." *Speak good English? English is my first language,* I think to myself. Really? Sometimes I can't begin to imagine what people are thinking. I hear the question all the time, "How come you don't know Korean?" You are Korean. You should know your own language and culture. Well, if you are German or Swedish, how come you don't know that language? It is kind of the same thing. I am adopted. Sometimes people ask me, "What does it feel like to be adopted?" I don't know. What does it feel like to not be adopted? "How can she or he be your parents? They don't look like you. If I'm only with one parent, people assume the other one is Asian and I'm half Asian. People say, "Oh you must be half." What does that mean? Like my mom is Asian and my dad is not or my dad is Asian and my mom is not. People say, "So you don't speak Korean? You don't speak Korean at home?" No, I don't have parents that speak Korean. Oh, so where were you born? Seoul, South Korea. I see, but you don't know Korean. No, my parents are Caucasian and they adopted me when I was six months old. Oh, I see. Do you think about Korea? No, I don't think about Korea. It is not something I think about on a daily basis.

These are some of my daily conversations with people that don't know me.

I found people to be disappointed that I don't know my Korean language. As I matured, I realized that, that is their problem, not mine. I am proud of knowing a few words here and there. Someday I will learn more.

Where do I fit in? There are so many unknowns in adoption. I didn't know where to go. At times, I struggled with my identity as a Korean adoptee through issues of attachment, abandonment, and relationships. What would life have been like if I weren't adopted? What would my life be like in Korea? Would the issues of grief and loss be relevant to me if I was in Korea? Sometimes it is hard for me to even imagine that I had a life in South Korea before coming to America. Yet, I did. It is a weird feeling, a feeling of not knowing, uncertainty. Not knowing your past, not knowing where you belong, and not knowing your identity. It is something that we as adoptees struggle with as we try to find 'our home.'

Issues of attachment, abandonment, relationships, and loss are all real to adoptees. These are all areas I didn't think I would struggle with coming to America as a baby. Yet, they are real. There is an inherit part of me that longs to know my birthparents, my culture, and my history. There is loss that can't be replaced. Having people talk about their families or culture can bring up emotions of loss. It is a struggle as I age but realize I am who I am.

While it can be hard as an adoptee, I have come to realize that family is family no matter where you are from. Your DNA is a part of you and so are the people that love, support, and raise you. I am grateful to have my incredible parents for their bravery and courage as well as my birthmother for her bravery and courage in giving me up. I can't even imagine how hard that must have been. Family is not just blood, it is who is there and who means the most to you. As an adoptee, I feel as though I have multiple people that are a part of my family. It goes along with being an orphan. We are always someone's family.

At the root of it, I wanted to be like others. However, at the end of the day, when I look in the mirror, I will see a Korean looking face/body. No matter how differently I color my hair, or put different color contacts in my eyes, or get plastic surgery, I will always look Korean. I am Korean. It has been a challenge to embrace that identity: an identity that I am still trying to learn more about.

All I wanted was to fit in. To be normal. To blend in. To not be different. To assimilate to American culture. If only people could walk in my shoes for once; if people could understand the complexities of adoption. Adoption is a life-long journey. If people could treat others with the utmost respect and dignity and without ignorance. If people could understand the two worlds adoptees live in every day. If people could understand that there are many stories of adoption: the adoptee, the birth parents, and the adoptive parents. If people could walk in the shoes of those adopted. There would be hope.

I am adopted. I was six months old when I came to Minnesota. I have gone to culture camp. I love spicy food, am inspired by martial arts, and love playing guitar and sleeping on the floor. I still have hope that one day more people will 'get it.' Adoption is a complex deal and a life long journey. It will always be a part of who I am.

As I have matured in age, many questions dwell in me of my past. Who am I? Where did I come from? One thing I know for sure is that I am learning more about what it means to be a Korean American and a Korean adoptee. My life is caught between two cultures. There is the American culture, and even though I've lived here basically my whole life, I will never fully fit in. There is the Korean culture. Although I have never been to Korea, I don't think I would feel totally accepted there, either.

I embrace both cultures, and it gives me hope

that I came to America. I am beyond grateful for my adoption and coming here. I am beyond grateful to my birth mother and her bravery in giving me up for adoption. I am beyond grateful for my adoption agency for placing me with such an amazing home. I am beyond grateful to my parents, who love me and raised me. It was hope that helped me overcome knowing who I am. It was hope.

Chapter 5:
Mysterious Diagnosis

"Fix You" - Coldplay

Growing up, my gross motor skills were lacking. I couldn't do the same things my peers could do. No matter how hard I tried, I wasn't able to do physical tasks the other kids my age did. I would try to walk, run, and jump as much and as far as others, but I couldn't. I could only walk a few feet at a time and then I'd reach my tiny little arms high in the sky and cry out, "Daddy carry, Daddy carry." I simply could not go any farther. My feet and legs got sore and I was done. My dad carried me wherever we went—on his shoulders or on his back—for many years, until I was too heavy for him to carry.

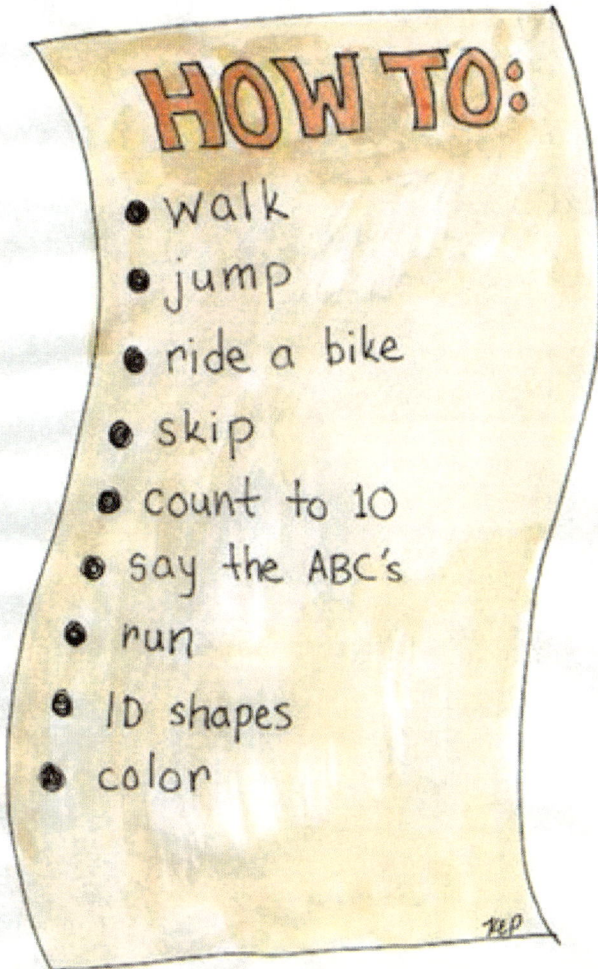

HOW TO:

- walk
- jump
- ride a bike
- skip
- count to 10
- say the ABC's
- run
- ID shapes
- color

It was like having a preschool teacher give me a list of skills that a student was expected to be developing at that age. I was just not developing them. I struggled to do many physical activities the other children could do. As a young child, I remember playing with the neighborhood kids and my preschool classmates. They would outrun me. I hated any games that required running, especially freeze tag, as I was always caught. I often found myself saying, "Wait for me!" I tried so hard to keep up with the others. All I wanted was to be 'normal' and to fit in. Sometimes I wanted to give up. However, I am a fighter and fought on.

In preschool, we had Bike Day. This was a special day in which all the kids brought their bikes to school and rode them around the playground. I had a bike. I was able to ride it, but just for a short period of time. When my legs gave out, I stopped my bike and waited. It was as though something was wrong with me. But what? My body cramped up and my heart raced. It was scary. I had to adapt my ways. With a creative brain, I was determined to do what I could to participate in this special day. I was the gas station

attendant, filling up the other kids' bikes with pretend gas as they drove off. I loved this job, and it made me feel accepted, wanted, and needed. To this day, I can't ride a bike. It takes too much energy.

My parents could see that I was not a 'normal' kid, and these problems continued to persist. It became apparent that there was a problem, but what? I don't remember what I might have thought at that time, but I did know that I longed to be healed. We went to practically every doctor in the Twin Cities area to diagnose my problem. My life was *already* consumed with doctors and medical care professionals—before the age of five! When people ask what I remember of my childhood, the most vivid memories are the doctor visits. The dreaded waiting rooms. Magazines galore. The waiting time before we could see the doctor. The smell of newly cleaned rooms. The sounds of adults discussing diagnoses and what to do with me. The fake smiles on the medical professionals' faces. The Gameboy I slipped into my back pocket to play while waiting. The wait. The tests. New faces coming in and out of rooms, asking questions. It was all questions and tests. I loved school and disliked missing school to go to a doctor's appointment. It seemed as though I had one appointment after another for weeks upon weeks, months upon months, and years upon years.

My life was consumed with doctor's appointments. My parents took so much time off work to take me to those appointments. I dreaded the thought of seeing another doctor. It seemed like it was a never-ending cycle. Many times, there would be no answers. A bunch of testing—but no answers. As I got older, I thought it was silly to keep this up. I felt like a guinea pig. They just wanted to test me for various things every so often with no real answers. I ran on a spinning wheel—test after test without getting off the wheel.

Every time I went to the doctor, it was the same thing: "Touch your toes. Breathe normally while I listen to your heart. Stick out your tongue and say 'Ah-hhh.' Walk up and down the hall." I could tell at a young age that this was going to become a huge part of my life. I was not looking forward to the 'ride' of doctor visits.

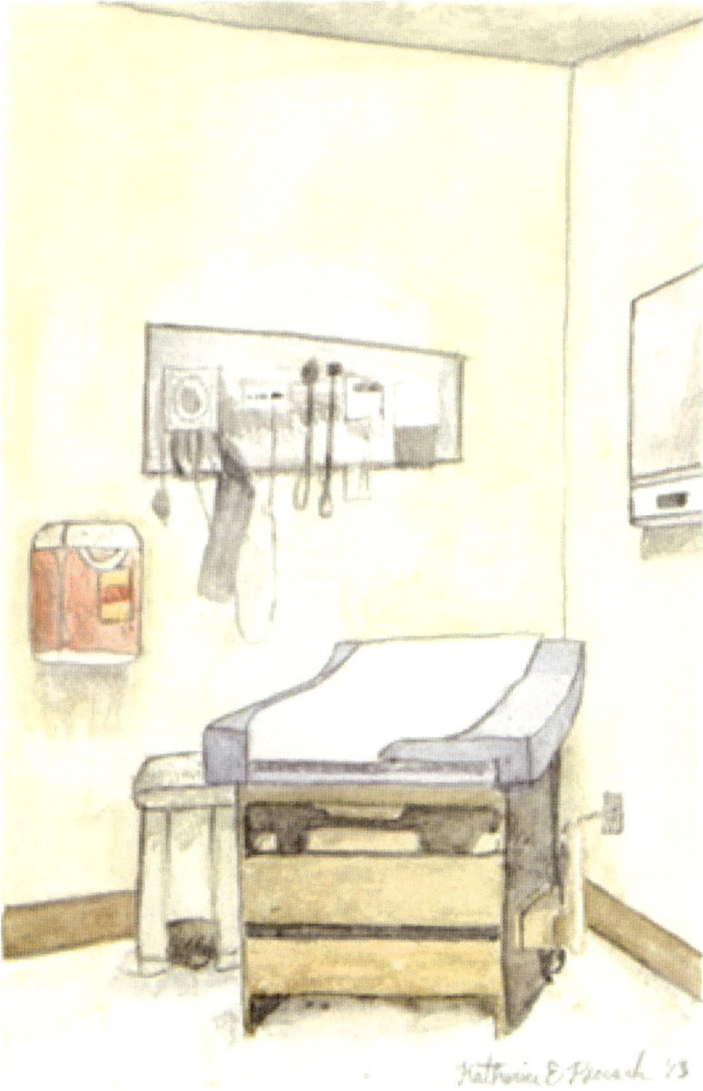

Katherine E. French '13

New diagnoses and approaches were being sought out. When I got to the age of five, a doctor decided our next step, and this important step would determine my future. My parents were excited to hopefully get some answers. I had no idea what was going on, except I was seeing yet another doctor who wanted to do more testing. This was my first operation, in which I had to hold still, drink some medicine that knocked me out, and they would proceed by cutting away some of my bicep for a muscle biopsy. The muscle biopsy would be the answer—at least this is what we had thought. It was worth a shot. We had doctors telling us that 'it' could be early stages of cerebral palsy to muscular dystrophy. The list went on and on, with various speculations. My parents were anxious to hear what this mysterious condition might be making my muscles tire so easily. All we could do was trust: trust in the doctors, and trust that it would be okay. It was a dark and scary time for my family as we waited for the results of the various tests.

The scar from the biopsy formed the shape of a slug. Every time I looked at it, the scar reminded me of everything I couldn't do, my weaknesses, and that my life was becoming a series of can'ts.

This slug, however, saved my life. It was what diagnosed my condition. The doctor suggested we fly to New York, to see, yet another, doctor: this time a specialist in mitochondrial diseases. Before I knew it, my parents and I were off on a plane to a specialist at Columbia University in New York, NY for their official diagnosis, discoveries, and expertise. I'm not sure as a young child I could comprehend or want to know about what I was going to be told. What they were about to tell me would rock my world. They told us that I had mitochondria myopathy—a rare muscle disease.

What in the world was that? My parents had never heard of it. In fact, the condition was only identified a few years before my diagnosis. Sure, we'd heard of some of the other conditions they told us about, but not this one. I guess it is pretty rare. Oh, and get this: many people with this condition die in their teens or twenties. Well, there's a lot of hope; I was six. Back in the early 90s, there was not nearly as much information about it, and there still isn't much. There are still many things we don't know or understand. All I really know is that it affects my muscles on a daily basis, giving me extreme muscle weakness in every part of my body.

During this time, we saw several different doctors. Many of the doctors didn't know how to help me or what to do. One of them in particular was most memorable. My parents and I were sitting in the doctor's office when the doctor turned to my parents and told them I would die around the age of fifteen or sixteen. "Take good care of her, and cherish the moments you have with her," he remarked. At almost six years old, I understood what that meant. I thought I was going to die at that age. It was interesting. From there on out, I started to live differently. I was trying to live in the present as much as a six year old could. I remember playing funeral with my dolls: having one of the dolls die and the rest come around her saying nice things about her. This went on for several months. Soon, I realized what it meant to live in the present and not to be anxious about what the future may hold. What was I supposed to do? At that point, my parents and I thought I only had ten years to live. How would you live if someone told you that? To this day, doctors can't believe that I am still alive or the fact that I am doing so well. Many consider it a true miracle.

Remember the slug? Well, it serves as a symbol that, whenever I look at it, not only is a scar of can'ts, but a scar of what makes me—me. For my parents, it gave them hope for treatment and an eventual cure. For me, it meant another battle to overcome.

Because of the mitochondria diagnosis, the doctor gave me a list of what I could *not* do.

1.   I would not be able to play many sports. No swimming across the lake. No bike riding, swimming, skiing, skating, soccer, or basketball. All good Minnesota sports were going to be a challenge for me. Despite my love for sports and fitness, I knew I would not become a jock, as much as I wished I could.

2. I couldn't do everyday things all my friends could do, either. There were many summer camps or after school activities I couldn't participate in

with the risk of overdoing it, especially those related to sports and physical activity.

3.   I could not drink caffeine. No Coke, Mountain
Dew, or Dr. Pepper; only decaf drinks.
Thank God for my Caribou *decaf*
Coffee.

This is not easy for a little kid.
Remember, I was in kindergarten when
this started.

I had a list of things I couldn't do,
but I also had a list of things I *could* do
and *had to* do. The list consisted of
some of the following things:

1.   I had to go to *many* more 'not so fun' doctor's
appointments; I dreaded going.

2.   I had to go through numerous exhausting tests.

3.   I had to take various medications and vitamins,
which were all really a guessing game and continue to be.

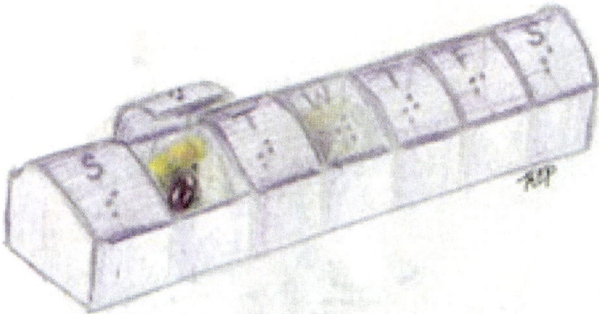

4.   I had to rest and take it easy.

5.   I had to eat every few hours to keep my energy and metabolism up. I have a high metabolism,
and it is very hard for me to gain weight. Even as

a child, I'd eat as much as a teenager and never retained that weight. There was even a time in which people thought I was emaciated because I didn't gain weight and was so skinny, no matter how much I ate.

6. I had to use a handicapped parking spot.

7. I had to use a wheelchair when walking far distances. That is a struggle within itself.

8.   I used the elevator in buildings to get to where I needed to go.

9.   Some exercise was necessary, but it was usually a struggle.

I still have these problems; they haven't gone away. It is not easy, but it is something I live with and deal with on a daily basis.

We learned that my body is frail. Any injury or illness would prevail longer than the average. We realized that my body has its limitations. It became a daily battle for me: keeping up with doctor's appointments, resting, and making sure I was doing what I needed to. For all I knew at that time, I was with people that didn't look like me, sleeping in beds, and there was a bunch of medical testing to be done.

With these devastating and life-changing results, not knowing exactly where to turn, and coming to grips with no cure for the diagnosis, it was natural for my parents to start to begin a search for my birth parents, to find out their medical history. Through the Children's Home Society, we searched for an answer. We searched and had hope that we would find my birth mother and she would be open to sharing her medical history and life with us. Was my condition one I got from her or my father? Neither? As I said, there was hope. It was not what we expected. We ended up with very few answers. Not the answers we looked or hoped for.

This is something that, as a young child, I could not comprehend. What I did know at the age of six was that this was going to be a long road ahead, telling others (school teachers, friends, family, doctors, etc.) about my medical condition. As I matured to my adult years, there was a desire to know more about my Korean life and what I 'left behind,' yet the mystery still remains. People say "home is where the heart is." I feel

that my home is in Bloomington, MN, and I am grateful for that. Seoul was where I was born. I have some
Korean traits in me, yet I am fully American.

Chapter 6:
One Thing after Another

"Blessed are those that persevere under trial, because when they have stood the test, they will receive the crown of life that God has promised to those who love Him." - James 1:12

I will preface this chapter by saying this is a somewhat hard chapter to write and probably a challenging chapter to take in as well. It is one of the most significant chapters, not only of my book, but of my life. This book is about overcoming obstacles and choosing a hopeful, positive outlook, but there were hardships to getting there. Please read this chapter not with sadness or pity, but with courage that if I can do it, so can you. Living with a severe, relatively-unknown medical condition is not easy, nor fun, but if you can choose to live with a hopeful attitude it makes life much easier.

With my body being frail and energy slowly fading, there were going to be some gives and takes. I slowly learned that my body was older than I was. It grew tired more easily and presented many more complications because of it.

"You look fine," people would respond, while, my body slowly lost energy. Yeah, I may look fine, but I wasn't. I had much more underneath that people didn't know. It grew on me that people couldn't see past the fact that I was struggling when I *looked* fine. If you saw on me on streets, you would never know I had a disability. I am not trying to hide it, it is just not as apparent as some are. It for sure has rocked my boat. Knowing that, every day was a major battle for me. I fight every minute for energy and to find the best ways to conserve that energy throughout the day.

When I exceed my limitations, I get *huge* muscle foot and leg cramps. It is truly the worst feeling ever! Ladies—think of period cramps, but on a daily basis, twice as painful, and all over your body. The lactic acid builds up throughout the day, and I would be doubled over in excruciating pain with tight knots in my

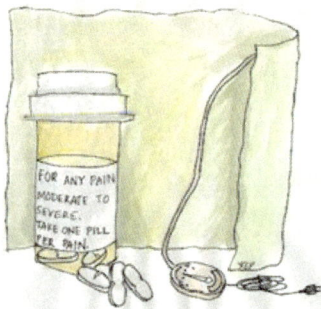

legs and feet. Walking for short distances feels like running a marathon for me. It is one the most painful experiences that occurs sometimes weekly, sometime daily. My energy and fatigue settled in quickly as I tried to go on and do more. It was as though my body tried to keep going and something was happening to make me stop. We later found out that the something was lactic acid buildup. Every time I use energy, lactic acid builds up. It is like the feeling of running a marathon, and it is so painful.

As a young child, I would get this often as I tried to keep up with my peers. I would lay awake at night in pain, unable to sleep, thinking, *Why me?* Why was I losing sleep over the pain in my legs and feet? I remember go into my parents' room, waking them up, and having them help me get Advil, water, and heating packs, and having them massage my feet. It took a while for the medication, heat packs, and massages to kick in and—finally—I was able to sleep. This happened often, and I still get these today. I wanted to have hope. How could I have hope when I was wide awake at night in much pain as an elementary school student?

I often describe this condition as running a marathon. I constantly have to evaluate how my body is doing energy wise. It is a condition in which lactic acid builds up very quickly. You know when you run a lot and your legs start to cramp up and hurt? I am sure many of you have experienced that before. Well, that is what I seem to experience on a daily basis. I have learned to live with this mito chondria disease, however, it's not fun. I do not wish this on anyone.

Well, anyway, back to the implications of this condition. There were many implications to endure with the mitochondria diagnosis. One of them was needing to use a wheelchair for long distances. When I got too big to ride in a stroller, I got a wheelchair. I remember having a little, red wheelchair growing up. We had the chair in the trunk of our car wherever we went, so no matter where we'd go, we were prepared. Because all the muscles in my body got tired, I was not able to push myself in the wheelchair. My parents or friends always pushed me around.

There were days that I was really tired from the night before, and this carried through the next day. I brought the wheelchair to school. On those days, I remember getting a never-ending amount of questions from other kids. Are you okay? What happened? Can I push you? Those were the most common questions. It was annoying, but at the same time a little nice to get so much attention from my peers. Some was out of care and concern.

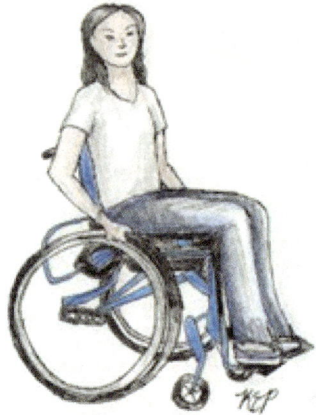

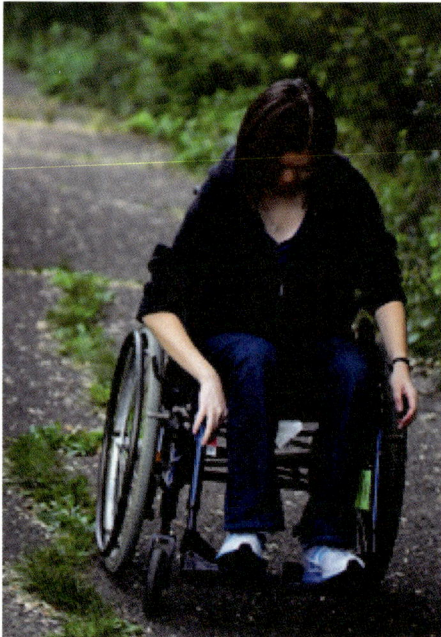

Riding in a wheelchair is a humbling experience. Anyone that rides in a wheelchair would probably agree that people treat you differently than an able-bodied person. When a person is in a wheelchair, he/she sits low to the ground. When you are lower, you see the world differently. Being in a wheelchair made me feel disabled. Even though I was, I didn't like that term and didn't like being so low. I felt less competent than others. It was as though people saw the wheelchair and immediately thought person with a disability, rather than me, Nikki.

People sometimes seem as if I am invisible to them. It irritates me when people don't stop to open or hold doors for those in wheelchairs. This happens a lot. It is like people don't see people in chairs and they let the door shut in their face. I am here, too! I feel so much more compassion than I would have without the wheelchair; I know what it is like and how I would like others to treat me. I see it from both perspectives: as a person that can walk and a person in a wheelchair. When I am walking without my chair, I feel abled and like I can take on the world. When I am in the wheelchair, I feel disabled and unable to do as much as others. While I am grateful to have a wheelchair, it is hard emotionally for me to be in it. Our society puts a stigma on people with wheelchairs and disabilities.

I have always been leery of traveling because it takes extra steps for me to arrange for my wheelchair. The thought it takes going on trips and every step in planning to make sure a room is accessible and available, let alone travel arrangements, is a headache. There are many countries and even states that are not wheelchair-friendly, especially those with bumpy and cobblestone roads.

Despite the struggle of being in a wheelchair, there are some plusses. Some people are not able to get out and walk and are wheelchair bound. I can get out of my wheelchair. When a person has a wheelchair, they often have a handicapped parking place. This often comes in handy at big events. One of the greatest features, in my opinion, is that I get to go ahead of the line for rides at Disney World or other venues. I feel privileged when I'm given special treatment like this.

Not many people know I use a wheelchair. It is not

something that comes up in daily conversation. Some close friends don't even know I use a wheelchair. It is nothing I try to hide; it is just not something people know about unless we go to an event or travel. It is always challenging to find people willing and able to push me in the wheelchair. I often don't want to be a hindrance to others or make others do heavy lifting with the wheelchair or make people push me. I hate getting the stares from people, like, "What's wrong with you?" and those who try to 'over help.' I also get people that don't understand or forget that I need a wheelchair to get around. Since I look 'normal,' people think I might have broken my foot or something. No matter how many times I get together with someone, they forget I need a wheelchair and it takes longer to get in and out of events. Sometimes I don't go places because it is too much of a hassle. It is another physical reminder to me of my health problems. I just want to be 'normal' and feel 'accepted.'

Another benefit, yet challenge, of this diagnosis is the privilege of having a handicapped parking sticker. This is what gave me hope. It gave me hope that I could participate in things I wanted to, by parking close to the entrance. It gave me hope to know that I could park closer and wouldn't get muscle cramps. It gave me hope. I am grateful for that. I am grateful that I can park closer to conserve energy. I am glad that I am able to have resources available to me. It gave me hope that I would be treated and viewed similar to others.

I have had a handicapped parking sticker ever

63

since I can remember. This was just a part of me. Having a handicapped parking sticker is not as easy as it may sound, though. Sure, it is nice to have when shopping on Black Friday when there are no parking spots available or when you are at a huge event; however, often times it comes with much grief. I have often gotten ugly, evil stares, dirty looks, shaking of heads, and even mean comments. It makes my heart cry to see discrimination thrown out to people that don't deserve this, especially when they are so young. I know I don't look like I need a handicapped parking sticker, but I do. It saves my life. I am able to participate in things I wouldn't otherwise be able to.

Two of these instances ring loud in my mind. This is an article I wrote for the local newspaper at the age of nine years old, describing my experience:

July 28, 1996

Hi! My name is Nikki Abramson. I am nine years old. I have a story to tell. On July 28, 1996, my family and I needed to go grocery shopping. At Byerly's, a bad person put a pick through my mom's car tire. When we drove off, we hit a curb. I was scared; so was my mom. We put our car by First Bank and hurried to the gas station to see if they could help us. They couldn't, so we called my dad for help. My dad and brother came right over. My dad put a tire on the car. We drove home to put the groceries away, followed by going to the police. That was my story. Oh, I'm handicapped, so the bad person looked at me and my mom and said, "They don't look handicapped," and did what I told you. We have to stick up for things like that. That was wrong. Think about it, a girl age nine and handicapped. How would you feel? I feel sad. I can't go on errands like I want. I want it to stop. It's not fair!

Thanks,

Nikki

So here I am, enjoying a trip to the grocery store as any nine year old would, and instead of having a pleasant afternoon, my mom's car tires get punctured because of someone's ignorance—someone thinking that we were not handicapped when we are. There was another time in which my mom and I were out running errands and a man walked up to us, saying in a threatening voice that we shouldn't be using a handicapped parking as that is for handicapped people. My mom and I started carrying a letter from my doctor to show to these angry people. I can't believe how rude people can be. By having this happen to me, it helped me to stand up for myself and learn to be my own advocate.

This happened to me, yet again, later in life. Another time in college when I was running late to a doctor's appointment, I parked in a handicapped parking place and rushed from my car to the office, not to waste more time and be later. When I came out to my car an hour later, I had a nasty note on my car windshield. It read:

"You should allow this spot for people who really need it. Stop taking the parking sticker from your grandma."

I thought to myself, *How rude. You do not even know my story.* Luckily, that was all that occurred. However, it was sad and disheartening as well. It makes me want to educate people even more on this issue, bring about awareness, change, and equality.

I feel as though every time I park in a handicapped parking place, whether I am alone or with others, I need to walk with a limp or walk in a weird way. I feel as though people are looking at me and judging me to see whether I am truly handicapped. I feel as though I always need to be on my best behavior and get out of the car when no one is around. There are times in which I literally sit in the car until I don't see many people around and get out of the car. I've waited for five minutes at one time just to get out of the car, so fewer people would see me. Why can't I just be me and

65

walk how I walk? I am sick of people judging me. I'd rather be safe than sorry, to protect myself.

Hope seemed to not be there. This idea of hope somewhere was lost. I couldn't understand what there was to hold on to when all I saw was darkness.

As I mentioned, there were numerous consequences of having a muscle disorder. In school, I got excused from gym class to rest. I felt horrible, seeing all my friends play the fun gym games while I sat on the sidelines to watch and cheer them on. This is not what I wanted. I participated in what I could without overexerting myself. My younger brother played soccer and ran track in school. It would kill me to see him play when I knew that I wouldn't have the joy of playing.

As if that wasn't bad enough, things didn't get any easier for me. In fact, they got more challenging the older I got. My muscles got weaker and weaker. In fourth grade, my teachers noticed that I had difficulty with my vision. "Nikki, can you see?" I responded "yes," however reading was difficult and my eyes got very tired easily. Teachers moved my desk to the front of the class, thinking that it would help. It did help, but there was still a problem with my eyes. We figured out that, due to lactic acid buildup, my eyes also got tired. Before I knew it, I ended up at the eye doctor.

After going through several eye doctors, many who didn't understand what I was going through, we finally found one that understood. He explained that I had astigmatism in both my eyes. You see, I have good vision. I don't really need glasses on a normal basis. However, because of the astigmatism and muscle weakness, I need glasses to see. I wear glasses for both reading and distance. I use the distance glasses when I'm driving, typing on the computer, watching TV, and other distance-related activities. I even wore them while doing sports or the arts to help me concentrate. I wear my reading glasses when I'm reading, so my eyes don't tire as easily.

I didn't mind wearing glasses. It did however make academics tough. In school, we had to read many pages a night. I always told people I didn't enjoy reading. Well, in reality, it wasn't true. It was more that my eyes grew weak so quickly that I could only read a few pages without getting a headache. You would think that as a writer, I would be an avid reader. Well, I am not. I don't think I have ever developed that drive because of my eye problems. When they are available, I used books on tape. As more of a visual learner, though, my mind often wanders when someone is reading to me. I try to find the best solution by taking as many breaks as possible when I read. I am grateful for glasses, though, giving my eyes a little break. It is like my 'cane,' helping me to see when my eyes have a hard time doing the job.

What number implication of a muscle disorder are we on? Never mind the number, here's the next. In fifth grade, we started studying geometry. At first, I hated geometry. With all subjects, we are good at some and not as good in others. We thought it wasn't my strong suit. As time passed, I realized that I struggled seeing the

shapes and patterns. I quickly and easily got frustrated with this, and wanted to 'throw in the towel.' I felt so lost and so discouraged that I didn't even want to try. No matter how hard I looked at the shapes and designs, I could not see it. I didn't understand why.

I could memorize all the proofs and geometric figures' names all I wanted, but telling you what they were was more of a challenge. I needed help, so I ended up back at the doctor's, this time for more testing. We were tossed between several doctors with various conclusions and even more testing, causing me to miss even more school and get more and more behind. With a few months or so worth of testing, I was diagnosed with another disability. This time it was a learning disability. It's called visual spatial disability. Another disability? Really? *Really?* Isn't having what I already had enough? Well, having this disability means it is difficult to see various geometric shapes. Often people with mobility issues as a young child have difficulty with spatial relationships.

To this day, I get lost *very* easily. It is nearly impossible for me to read maps. I get so frustrated when people ask me for directions, as I don't know how to give them or read them. I can follow directions such as 'turn left on this street,' but when I'm trying to drive east, I have no way of knowing what direction that is. I couldn't tell you if a store is at the north or south end of the mall. When I look at a map, I have no idea what it is saying—not because I don't know how to read it, but because my brain doesn't process it that way. Once, I ended up going the wrong way returning from an appointment back to my house and needed to call my dad's secretary to help find where I was and navigate me back. If only I could have someone as my personal navigation system all the time. GPS is great, but not as good as a real person It can be frustrating and embarrassing for me to admit that I can't see geometric figures, understand directions, and see visual figures on a graph.

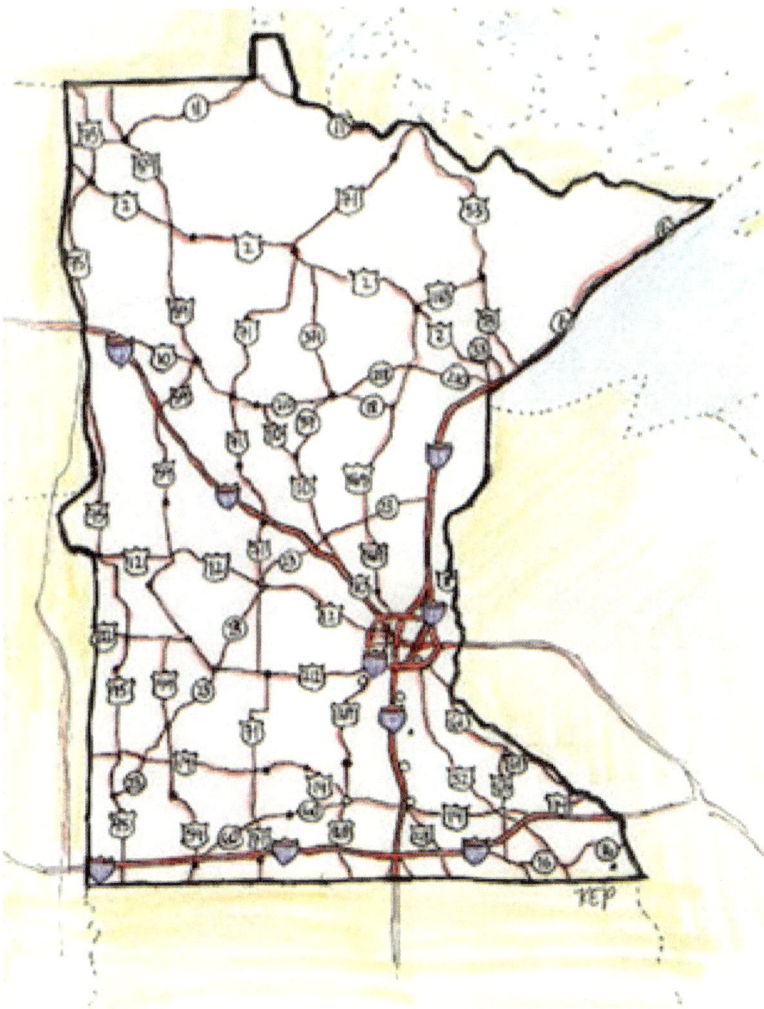

I failed geometry class *twice* and needed to retake the class. I felt as though I was a failure at times. Why didn't I get it? I even took a geometry-heavy college class and had to take it *twice,* as well. Where is hope when you are barely able to graduate from high school or barely able to graduate with the major you dreamed of? This tore me to the depths of my being. Why did I keep failing when I was trying so hard? I tried so hard to understand the material.

As my body matured with the complexities of health problems, so did my teeth. In fourth grade, I found out that braces were in the cards for me. I wasn't a fan of braces. Having to go every week to get them tightened. Having to brush a certain way. Not being able to eat certain foods, like caramel apples in the fall or corn on the cob in the summer. More 'can'ts' were added to my list.

Oh, and who can forget having a retainer that you had to take out when you ate and had to wash every day? There was the dreaded folding up the retainer in a napkin and trying not to forget it and throw it in the garbage at the end of a meal. Anyone? Anyone? Well, much like my personality, I ended up with braces *twice*! I guess my teeth couldn't figure out how to be straight. Overcoming the celebration of having your braces off and then being told you need them again, a year or so later, is not what you are looking for—for your bank account or your mouth. I have now worn glued-in retainers for the past thirteen or so years. It is nice not having to take them in and out.

Fourth grade was a challenge, fifth grade was a challenge, and yet sixth grade hit me with another challenge: another medical problem with my already-frail body. At my yearly check-ups, my primary care doctor asked me to bend down. I proceeded to do so. This time was different. She stepped back and thought for a moment and said "You need to have a specialist look at your back. It looks like you might have scoliosis."

Scoliosis? What is that? She went on to explain that my back was curved into an S formation and that they needed to correct it before it got worse. It would either be a back brace or surgery. Before I knew it, I was at an orthopedic doctor getting numerous x-rays of my back and spine. It was indeed scoliosis, and that meant I had a huge curvature of my spine. In fact, it was just a few degrees away from surgery. After consulting other doctors about the process, my parents and I opted out of surgery due to mitochondria myopathy and decided to go the brace route to protect my spine from getting even more crooked.

The back brace was a huge piece of white plastic that had Velcro straps attached to it. Getting the brace made was a process within itself. They put Paper-Mache around my body and molded a hunk of plastic to strap from my neck to my pelvis. They expanded the brace every year as I matured and developed, and I ended up wearing the brace for four years. *4 years!*

Now, wearing a brace is not fun.

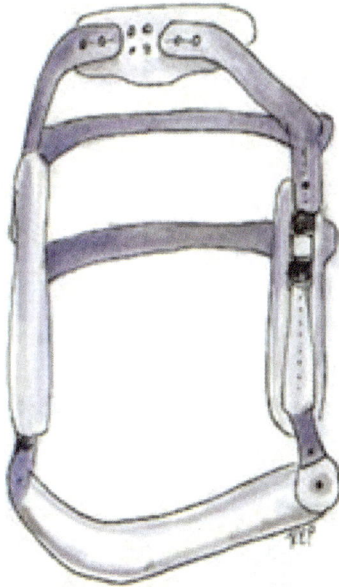

It was hot, sticky, and itchy. Sometimes I found myself so sweaty because I had this huge chunk of plastic on my body that I couldn't take off no matter how uncomfortable and gross it was. It was uncomfortable to sleep in. I only got one hour a day to take it off, meaning I wore it for twenty-three hours a day for four years. The hour I got off was to shower and allow my body to breathe. Taking it off was a huge sigh of relief, allowing my body to be free again. Every time I hugged someone, people would ask what that big, pokey thing was. I felt like a turtle, with the shell protecting my body in the brace, and wanted to hide myself from others. It was a huge self-esteem factor for me, as I hated wearing it. I hated the way I looked and felt.

Because I wore the brace so much, I had to give up many things I loved…including a sport that I could participate in—karate. I gave up my passion, karate, to heal and correct my spine. Buying clothes was one of the hardest things. I had to buy a whole new wardrobe to fit over the hunk of plastic around my petite frame. I remember needing to buy a size bigger than I was to hide and fit over my brace. I didn't want anyone to know I wore it unless they had to.

After I got the brace off, I participated in years of physical therapy throughout high school and college to strengthen my spine and back. Going to physical therapy gave me hope. It gave me hope that my back would get stronger. I had a great team of physical therapists at Gillette Children's that helped get me back on track. With scoliosis, my back constantly hurts. I have bought many lumbar supports, chairs, and massages to help. To this day, I get x-rays of my back and spine once a year to make sure everything continues to look good. It continues to be a never-ending cycle.

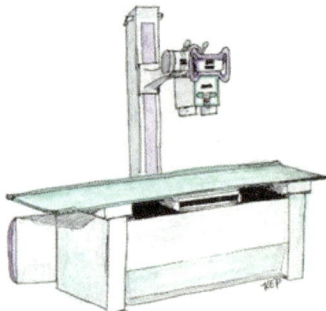

Eighth grade presented another hurdle in my life. Because my muscles fatigued, so did my lungs, and I developed asthma. At times, it felt as though an elephant was sitting on my chest. I felt like I was breathing through a straw and couldn't get enough air in my lungs. Every few months I developed asthma attacks. Going in to see the pulmonologist twice a year and having to wear nose plugs to do breathing tests does not work well with Asian noses. I had many asthma attacks, especially in high school and college, causing me to miss many days of school. There were days the asthma got so bad I didn't know what to do. I felt like I was going to die; there was no air coming in. The airways were so restricted, and all the doctors could do was give me Prednisone, which made my body even weaker. I have a list of medications a mile long for the asthma, and honestly I am not sure what exactly was or wasn't helping.

Wherever I go, I need to carry an inhaler. Asthma still gives me problems today. I try to do what I can to prevent asthma attacks, but it can be quite scary. You never know when you will be hit with one. Because I have such low muscle strength, it is a challenge for me to use an inhaler, so I get nebulizer treatments instead. I am grateful that this type of technology is available to help me to breathe just a little bit better.

Along with the asthma came a bunch allergy triggers, including trees, mold, pollen, grass, horses, penicillin, peanuts, and shellfish. So, on top of carrying around an inhaler, I also carry an epi pen in case of anaphylactic shock. Thankfully, I have never had to use that. With all the environmental allergies, it was recommended that I get allergy shots once a week. While this gave me hope that my allergies would get better and my asthma would lessen, the number of doctor visits increased to seeing a medical care professional once a week. Every time I saw my doctor, I was reminded and asked if I had my inhaler and epi pen with me.

Year after year, it seemed like my list of obstacles was getting bigger and bigger. This mitochondria disease presented itself with lots of physical complications. All I wanted was to be accepted, normal, and stronger. There were more and more things I had to watch for. My health became a daily battle. I had to watch everything from my sleeping, eating, and energy level, to not overexerting myself. This was a challenge and often continues to be one. All I could do was overcome.

With mitochondria disease, I needed to make sure I ate well. I needed to eat every four hours. I often brought snacks wherever I went. I even had school accommodations to eat in class if I needed to or leave class early to make sure I got ahead in the lunch line. I had a huge metabolism. I ate like a teenage boy and didn't gain much weight. I had a period of time in which people thought I was emaciated and that my parents weren't feeding me enough.

My body also reacted to extreme conditions, both heat and cold, causing me to not enjoy the outdoors at certain temperatures. Too hot or too cold would often make me sick, and I had a hard time staying in places at those temperatures. Because of this and living in Minnesota, I stay inside much of the time.

This rare condition causes me to get sick often.

Most people get sick with a cold that lasts a few days. For me, it lasts a week and half—up to a month. I missed quite a bit of school and work as I got hit twice as hard as others with anything and everything that I came in contact with. Strep throat, colds, flu, allergies...you name it. Because of all of this, I needed to make sure I was getting enough sleep and be sure to keep up with my medications. Both were constant reminders from my pediatrician and my parents.

Despite all that was going on with all these medical conditions and issues and how frustrating my medical history was, I wanted to be more than my limitations. So I pushed myself. I worked out in gym class, played tennis after school, and tried to keep up with everyone else. Never mind that mitochondrial diagnosis, I was determined to be 'like everyone else.' As soon as I overdid something, my body became cold and stiff, and I was unable to move. My lips turned blue and my parents knew at that moment I had 'overdone' it. Sadly, I ended up in the ER. Near death with IV bags dripping saline in my arms. Drip, drip, drip. I heard the liquid flowing through the bags into my arms. Every ten minutes, the blood pressure cuff squeezed my arm and beeping happened.

For hours upon hours, I lay on my back, looking up at the dropped ceiling, the dead bugs they hadn't cleaned out, and I had to wonder, why me? I wondered if I was going to die. Hearing the doctors talk outside my room was annoying, and I couldn't quite make out what they were saying. It seemed as though they didn't have any answers. The TV was on, but nothing ever happens at 1:00 in the morning. Trust me, kids, go to bed!

This happened to me not once, not twice, but three times. I wanted so badly to have hope; hope in something that was greater than me. Hope that I would live and be healed. I longed to feel accepted and be more like my peers. We all do. It took me a while to figure out I could have hope and still 'be me.'

Upon many doctors' visits of various types for my conditions, I quickly realized that I had seen someone from almost every medical system in the Twin Cities, including the famous Mayo Clinic. Every time I went to a doctor, I was given a bunch of forms to fill out. These forms are all similar. They all ask for one thing in particular that I never know how exactly to answer. Should I cross it out? Should I leave it blank? Should I write 'I don't know' or 'unknown'? This question asks for my medical history. They ask if my parents had any type of conditions to be aware of. I respond with my initials N/A, Nikki Abramson, or not applicable; I don't know my medical history. It is unknown. No information. None! Zip! Nada! I was adopted! Sure, I would love to know what my birth parents' genes were and if I am susceptible to getting something, but I don't know. I have hope that one day I will know more to indeed put down something on the medical forms instead of a huge "X" over the page and saying N/A. It remains a mystery.

Despite the mystery of this, I had one person, one doctor, who truly invested in me—my well-being, my health—but also me as a person. Dr. Angie Thompson Busch, my pediatrician, pushed me on to success. I saw her most of my life. Even when I was too old for her pediatric practice and clinic, she still saw me. She allowed me to see her even though I was an adult, as she 'got it'; she understood it. She knew me and made me feel comfortable. I was able to share anything with her. I think she was one of the only people in my life that knew almost anything about me. She was one of the doctors that I didn't dread seeing. In fact, it was nice (at times) to get sick, so I could see her.

She always knew what to do and, if she didn't, would research it. Dr. Busch was not afraid of my condition; it spurred her to learn even more. I admire her and am glad to have had one constant doctor in my life through the ups and downs. Dr. Busch was there. She gave me the hope. When I thought I was 'dying,' she gave me the confidence I needed. I am beyond grateful for the ways she has been a part of my life.

All I wanted was to fit in. To be normal. To blend in. To not be different. To not be disabled. To not have to ask for adaptations. If only people could walk in my shoes for once. If only people could understand the complexities of living with a disability, a life-changing one, a rare one, and one that remains a mystery. One that you don't know how you will feel on any given day. Having a disability is not easy. Rather, it is a lifelong journey. If only people could treat others with utmost respect and dignity and without ignorance. If people could understand the two worlds I live in as a person that is disabled. Living like many people and living with life-threating conditions every day. If only people could understand that there are many stories of people with disabilities and many complications on a daily basis. If only people could walk in the shoes of those that have a disability. What is normal? Don't judge; don't assume.

MEDICAL HISTORY

1. Have you had any previous medical history? ☐YES ☐NO ☒ N/A

2. If yes, please mark if you or any relatives have had any of the following:

AIDS/HIV	☐YES ☐NO	EPILEPSY	☐YES ☐NO	OSTEOPOROSIS	☐YES ☐NO
ALCOHOLISM	☐YES ☐NO	FRACTURES	☐YES ☐NO	PARKINSON'S	
ALLERGIES	☐YES ☐NO	GLAUCOMA	☐YES ☐NO	DISEASE	☐YES ☐NO
ANEMIA	☐YES ☐NO	GONORRHEA	☐YES ☐NO	PSYCHIATRIC CARE	☐YES ☐NO
ANOREXIA	☐YES ☐NO	GOUT	☐YES ☐NO	R. ARTHRITIS	☐YES ☐NO
ASTHMA	☐YES ☐NO	HEART DISEASE	☐YES ☐NO	STROKE	☐YES ☐NO
BLEEDING		HEPATITIS	☐YES ☐NO		
DISORDERS	☐YES ☐NO	HERPES	☐YES ☐NO	SUICIDAL	☐YES ☐NO
BRONCHITIS	☐YES ☐NO	HPM		TUBERCULOSIS	☐YES ☐NO
BULIMIA	☐YES ☐NO	CHOLESTEROL	☐YES ☐NO	TUMOR GROWTHS	☐YES ☐NO
CANCER	☐YES ☐NO	KIDNEY DISEASE	☐YES ☐NO	ULCERS	☐YES ☐NO
CATARACTS	☐YES ☐NO	LIVER DISEASE	☐YES ☐NO	OTHER	
CHICKEN POX	☐YES ☐NO	MEASLES	☐YES ☐NO	_____	
DIABETES	☐YES ☐NO	MIGRANES	☐YES ☐NO	_____	

3. Injuries/Surgeries had: Description   Date

    FALLS _____

BEAD INJURIES _____

BROKEN BONES _____

DISLOCATIONS _____

SURGERIES _____

4. Any other information:

    No Past Records

Chapter 7:
Navigating through School

"I can do all things through Christ who gives me strength." - Philippians 4:13

How many of you had teachers who took time for you? I mean, really took time for you. How many of you had teachers who invested in you and truly believed you could do it, even when you didn't believe in yourself? I did, and I am beyond grateful for the amazing teachers, friends, and coaches that helped me throughout my years of schooling. As much as I loved school, school and learning were a challenge for me. Much of my challenge was due to a visual-spatial disability and the muscles in my body fatiguing quickly.

As long as I can remember, I attended school. Shortly after coming to America, I attended an amazing daycare and preschool, Kinderberry Hill in Edina, MN. After preschool, I received education from one of the best and most challenging schools in the Twin Cities area. In fact, the school recently won an award for being one of the most rigorous schools in Minnesota. The small, private preschool through twelfth grade, college-prep school, International School of MN (ISM) in Eden Prairie, MN, was one of the most challenging, yet life-giving schools. I don't think I realized how thankful I was to have gone to ISM until after I graduated.

I started out as a shy kindergartener in 1992. With the help of many of the teachers and staff, I turned into a blossoming young woman and a proud graduate of The International School of MN in 2005. I loved this school! It prepared me not only for college, but for life, and gave me experiences I would never have gotten in a bigger public school. I call it a world-class education. In many ways, it was a great fit for me. Teachers cared about me and fellow students became lifelong friends. It was a safe environment where I could explore many areas.

Like I said, I loved school. I loved everything about it. I even loved wearing the school's gray, maroon, and white uniforms, as I didn't need to think about what I was going to wear that day. Everyone wore the same clothing. I didn't have to compete for looking the best. In fact, I often wear polos and gray pants today out of habit. Despite the many friends and teachers I had that were supporting me in every way, I still struggled academically. It was challenging, in every way, shape, and form. I remember notes from teachers (some of which I still have, starting in second grade): "Nikki works hard, but needs a tutor in math." "Nikki needs to work on her handwriting." "Nikki's reading comprehension skills are lacking." "Nikki struggles with her math facts." It went on and on. It was a challenge that I was not going to give up.

There were times when I did want to give up. In fact, several years were so academically challenging for me, my parents and I school shopped. We looked for other schools where I might be able to succeed. I ended up attending the local public school twice, for a week each time, before realizing that it wasn't for me. I went to public school in fifth grade and seventh grade. We realized that it didn't give me enough of a challenge at the public school. I knew I wanted to overcome, but how? I worked hard, but I still didn't succeed. Why me? Why did it seem like no matter how hard I studied for a test, I would not do well? No matter how intensely I paid attention in class, took notes, asked questions, went to tutor labs, and asked for help, I still did not grasp the material as some of the other students did. This was a daily frustration for me. I so badly wanted to be 'smart.' For some students, the material just clicked. They barely studied and did well. I was not one of those students. This was another hurdle and challenge I would need to overcome—my self-confidence and a belief that I could do the work and would be successful.

There were struggling times and really dark periods when I didn't think I would ever pass certain classes. I remember coming home distraught, thinking I would never understand things, no matter how many hours I studied. Were academics always going to be this hard? In the end, I stayed at The International School through my high school years, and with my determination, hard work, diligence, and drive succeeded, passed, and graduated. In fact, despite being the most challenging, they were also the most rewarding years.

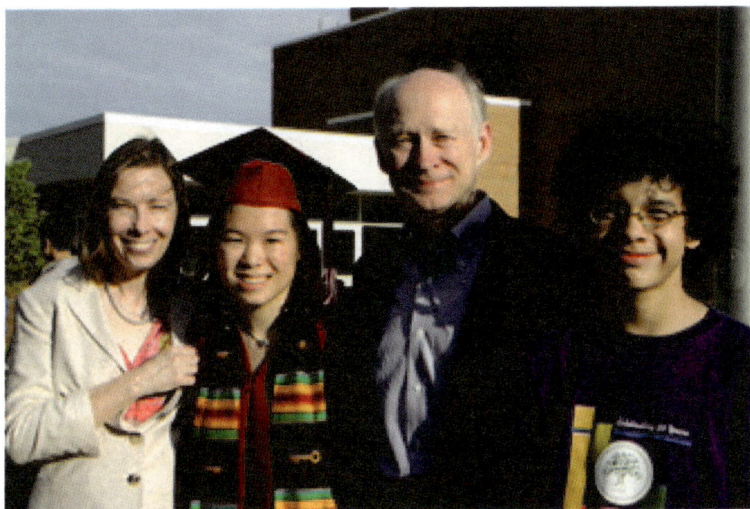

I think some of what helped my confidence were the notes on my report cards. Here are some things that my teachers said about me:

First Grade: Nikki is showing a nice improvement in all her work. She is contributing to discussions and gaining self-confidence.

Fourth Grade: Nikki is a serious, conscientious student. She strives to do her best.

Sixth Grade: Nikki always strives for excellence. Her inquisitive mind and commitment to her studies makes her a role model. The results reflect her fine attitude and tireless effort. A highly-motivated, responsible, and conscientious student, Nikki works diligently and produces excellence. She is well-liked and respected by students and staff.

Seventh Grade: Nikki takes her education seriously and made significant academic improvement. With her attitude and effort, Nikki will be able to achieve her goals. Keep up the good work. She always strives for excellence and her inquisitive mind and commitment to her studies makes her a role model. She is respectful, well mannered, and always ready to be of service.

Eighth Grade: Nikki has struggled this year, but hasn't given up. She is an all-around student who works hard inside the classroom and out, always striving to understand the material in great depth to do her best. She is diligent, prompt, and generous. She is a joy to teach and a source of pride at ISM! Nikki is highly motivated and well-liked by others. ISM is a better place because of her commitment to our school and willingness to serve.

Ninth Grade: Nikki works very hard and her effort pays off. It usually takes some time for her to grasp a concept, but once she understands she does quite well. Nikki is respectful of others, well-mannered, and always ready to be of service.

Tenth Grade: Nikki is a diligent student and a pleasure to have in class. She works well with other students. Nikki has an excellent attitude and displays a positive demeanor at all times! She is a student who wants to do well. When she puts forth effort, her results are quite good. She works very hard with a strong work ethic and comes in regularly for help. She must *not* get discouraged. Persistence is rewarded.

Eleventh Grade: The results this year reflect her attitude and tireless effort. A highly-motivated, responsible, and conscientious student, Nikki works diligently on school assignments. She is well-liked and respected by all. Her involvement in Student Life is outstanding! Nikki is diligent and is a pleasure to have in class. She assumes a positive leadership role within the classroom. Nikki is a role model for other students. She is respectful, demonstrates a high level of compassion to others, and is always willing to help out. She puts forth the effort needed to achieve good results.

Twelfth Grade: Nikki is a role model for other students. She is a diligent student and a pleasure to have in class. She is capable, helpful, and enjoys participation. Her frequent absences due to illness were concerning, but with Nikki's commitment and follow through she is still able to achieve. The results Nikki received this year are an accurate reflection of her fine attitude and tireless effort. She is well liked and respected. We wish Nikki well at Bethel University!

All these positive report cards, quotes from teachers, and remarks made me feel that I could overcome these academic challenges and hurdles. Despite my sometimes low grades, it gave me hope that the teachers and administrators saw effort, diligence, and determination. For several years I was on the academic honor roll: sixth, seventh, and twelfth grade. In seventh grade, I made the National Junior Honor's Society. It was a huge honor to receive this type of recognition. My tireless effort did, in fact, pay off!

Despite my challenges, I earned two prestigious awards. In fifth grade, I earned the lower school Director's Award, and in the eleventh grade, I earned the high school Director's Award. This award is given for achievements, hard work, and contributions to the school. I could not believe it. Usually this award goes to someone who is that "all-around student," involved in everything with superb grades. Never would I have thought that it would go to me. The award is given as one of the last awards at the yearly Honors Convocation.

I remember that day exactly. It was a defining moment for me. One that helped define hope—hope in its essence. On the morning of Thursday, June 10, 2004, my mom said to make sure I wore an extra clean, crisp, unwrinkled uniform. I knew that it was our annual Honors Convocation, in which we celebrate students' achievements, but prior to her comment, it didn't occur to me that I would get an award. I thought perhaps I would be getting an award for my dedication to the Student Life program (which is similar to student government), but I never thought I would get the award I was about to receive.

Having been asked to speak about Student Life at the ceremony, I thought about my speech and what my team had been working on all year long. I was proud of them, and my heart beamed to share what we accomplished. When I arrived at the auditorium packed with students grades four through twelve, teachers, and parents, I quickly noticed my parents. I said, "Hi, what are you doing here?" They said they were "asked to come."

Still without giving it much thought, I took my seat. I gave my speech and awards were passed out. At the end of the ceremony, they proceeded with the final award—The Director's Award. As I mentioned, the Director's Award is a prestigious award. It is an award I am truly honored and humbled to have received. Mrs. Berg, our school's director, stood up to speak, taking a deep breath with emotion-filling eyes as she read her description of the recipient. I was thinking to myself as she read the description, *Wow, this sounds like an amazing person*, and I started to guess who this award might go to.

Here is what she said:

"This student is one the most determined young people I have come in contact with as a seasoned teacher and administrator. Despite a serious physical condition that could impact physical strength and stamina, she perseveres like none other.

"As a preschool student in 1992, she made a smooth transition to ISM."

(Here I was thinking to myself who came in 1992.)

"One of her recommendations said, 'She exhibits creativity and ingenuity. She has many friends and plays well with them.' Throughout her early years and on through elementary school, she left her mark. She adjusted well to the rigorous curriculum, and because she has good work habits and the ability to make plans and carry them out in an orderly way, she has experienced academic successes. Even when the subject matter is difficult, she does not give up; in fact, she seems to dig deeper yet, dedicating extra time and effort to master the material.

"Her interests are wide and varied; as a result, she has contributed to ISM in meaningful ways. Musically, she has participated in concert choir and show choir. Also, she has played a range of characters in each of the theater productions at ISM. Not only is she an effective team player, she can take on a leadership role as she has done so effectively in our Student Life Organization. As the Deputy Head of Lower School—"

(Everyone was staring at me and beaming.)

"—she helped to coordinate activities throughout the year for the elementary students, most importantly the lower school Student Life trip to Duluth this past spring."

(At this point, I knew it was me.)

"She is an excellent role model for these blossoming young students as she is responsible and reliable. Her organizational skills put many of us to shame. She is admired.

"She accepts people for who they are; she is always respectful and sincere. As a student at International School of Minnesota, she has experienced a diverse school population that has prepared her well to approach life with an open-minded and tolerant attitude. She is a life-long learner with a thirst for knowledge and real life experiences.

"As Director of The International School of Minnesota, it is my pleasure to give The International School of Minnesota's Director's Award to Nikki Abramson."

What? Really? Me? As soon as she read my name, the *whole* auditorium—*students, teachers, and parents*—were on their feet. I could barely make my way up to receive the award as people were patting me on the back and giving me high fives as I walked up. My face felt like lava as I got on stage, embarrassed and honored. Good thing I didn't need to give a speech as I was so flabbergasted, I am not sure what I would have said. I gave Mrs. Berg a hug, shook her hand, paused for a picture, and took my award. As I hugged her, on the other side of the stage faced many of my teachers who stood by me over the years, all clapping and smiling. It felt as though I climbed a mountain. This from a school that I left twice due to academics and wasn't sure if I could succeed in.

That night the phone rang off the hook with people congratulating me. The next day, a friend had surprised me with a Fedex delivery of flowers. It was something I could not even begin to ask for. I will never forget that moment; that moment that hope settled into my very bones.

School was challenging for me. With my medical conditions and my muscles that tired easily, I needed many adaptations. Adaptations, like many things in life, are both positive and negative. For example, I got to use the school's elevators to get around the building. I even got to pick one person to ride in the elevators with me for the day. It was a highlight to ride the elevators, but frustrating when I was late for class because of it or when kids or staff asked, "Why do you get to use the elevators when others don't?" Soon students knew and accepted it.

My medical condition requires me to eat a good

lunch, one where I have plenty of time to eat a sub-stantial amount. As an elementary school student and even today, I eat like a teenage boy. I had an ac-commodation to leave class a few minutes early to eat lunch, giving me plenty of time to get my lunch and eat. With extreme temperatures, I needed to stay in-side for recess. I'd rather stay inside than go outside. Sometimes it made me feel special and privileged to be able to stay in from recess if I needed to.

This was a huge thing for me, as my arm got tired from writing answers or my eyes fatigued from read-ing. Because my eyes also grew tired easily, I had more accommodations. I got extra time for tests and pa-pers. This accommodation helped me perform better on tests, but often I missed out on free periods or after school activities due to having to finish tests. I also 'read' some of my school books on tape. This helped me so I didn't have to wear out my eyes reading pages and pages of text. It is difficult to be a visual learner, yet not have eyes that are able to read for extensive periods of time.

Due to my body reacting to extreme tempera-tures, I often got to stay inside for recess and became the teacher's helper. Perhaps this was a reason I wanted to become a teacher. Many days of the week, I stayed indoors for recess to help my teacher cut var-ious things out or put information in Friday Folders. This provided me with a glimpse of encouragement that I truly could overcome my disabilities and teach a class.

A favorite class for many students is gym class. I, too, liked gym class. As you can imagine, gym class produced some frustrations for me. I wanted to par-ticipate in the gym games and activities, and for the most part I was able to. I was excused from certain gym class requirements, such as running the dreaded mile or swimming class. I did what I could, though, and I compensated by partly running, partly walking, a quarter of a mile. I often finished a quarter mile around the time a few of my friends were finishing the whole mile. I was proud of what I could do, though. I would try to beat my own time, doing it my own way. I may not be like others, but I can set goals and succeed.

Despite gym being a struggle, I was fortunate to be able to participate in girls' softball in eighth grade. I played outfield and had a runner that ran the bases for me. I hit the ball and as soon as I hit, another player ran the bases. It felt good that I could participate in sports with others and be part of such a unique and special team. I also participated in weight training. By lifting as much as I could, I slowly gained muscle strength, energy, and endurance.

My greatest passion, though, was karate. I first took a class through the ISM after school program. I started National Karate lessons at six years old. I loved karate! I ate, slept, and breathed karate. It became my life and I spent many hours at the studio practicing. I put all my identity into that sport and competed in various competitions. I even said one day I would become a karate instructor. I was fascinated by the various forms we learned and the self-defense skills. I did what I could, and I learned to pace myself. It gave me great discipline. I achieved a brown belt in middle school. Although it was a tough decision, I quit karate because of the brace I wore for scoliosis. Through many adaptations and at a slower pace, I was able to participate in sports to a limited degree.

Particular subjects in school were difficult for me, specifically math and science. I remember as if it were yesterday when I was in eighth grade science. During every science class that year, I wanted to give up. I felt lost, as I didn't understand the material. It was like I was on a highway driving down the road, unable to find the correct turn.

My eighth grade science teacher, Amy Emanuelson Blaubach, saw something in me. Despite my frustrations, I put forth my best effort. Amy went above and beyond to help me. She took the time to meet with me before and after school. She once said to me, "my door is always open." That year I ended up with a final grade of 69%, one point shy of passing the class, but I was satisfied to know that I tried my hardest and never gave up. Despite my frustrations, I felt encouraged. One day, before tutoring me, Amy said some of the most profound words that would ring true in my mind forever: "I can do anything I set my mind to do."

As Amy and I exchanged notes of gratitude, I was struck by a few which said: "You have worked so hard in science all year and certainly came a long way. Just keep reminding yourself that you can do anything you set your mind to do. I wish you all the success and happiness—I know that with your determination you will accomplish your goals and dreams. You remind me why I love teaching. You are a caring person whom I am lucky to know. Remember those famous words from 8th grade—'You can do anything you set your mind to do.'" Amy believed in me. She instilled hope in me. This was one of the first times I felt I could achieve my dreams.

My teacher continued to mentor me throughout my high school career and beyond. When I struggled with other classes, I would write her an email saying, "It's so hard. I don't get it. I will never get into college." In one email she responded with, "Hang in there! Life isn't about tests. It's about doing the best you can with what you've got so that you can achieve your dreams! Schools and tests are just the roads that give you the tools so that you can become whatever you desire in the future." I took these words to heart. Life isn't about tests, but about achieving your dreams and having the hope that you can fulfill them. Her words encouraged me and gave me faith that I could do it. Today as I write these words, her words are on my bulletin board, pressing me on.

For one of my college essays, I was asked to write about an influential person in my life. I choose, Ms. Blaubach. I told her about my planned essay and asked her permission to write about her. She said, "No problem, Nik. I'd be happy to help you out any way I can, be it now or in the future. You have also influenced me in a positive way, too!" When I sent her the completed essay, she wrote back, "Your college essay has made me so happy! I don't know if you know this, but the greatest goal for a teacher is that over all the students that come through their door, they hope and pray that they can touch one, just one, life. To have you reference something I said to you years ago was really cool. It made me think that perhaps my goal of touching one person has come true. Thank *you* for being you."

My teacher, my mentor, my role model, became my friend. Amy tutored me throughout some courses in college and was a wonderful supporter. I went to her wedding and she attended my college graduation. Amy even hired me for my first job out of college. It was such an honor, and I am so grateful for her in helping me along my way. Ms. Amy Emanuelson Blaubach gave me hope. The hope that I could do it. I could teach; I could be successful, and life would be good. I am forever grateful for her support and belief in me.

In ninth grade, I wrote about my eighth grade experiences during journal time in English class. I am not able to tell you what the writing prompt was, but I was deeply moved by it and wrote this:

"Science is really hard for me. This made me frustrated and angry. I really didn't know what to do. Science never clicked like English and Spanish. I got those and they always came easy to me. Every night studying I felt like I should give up and it would never ever come. I felt like I wouldn't succeed in anything.

"This last year in 8th grade, I had Miss Emanuelson, and she taught me to never give up and always keep positive. I kept praying about it and working hard, and the last science final clicked and I understood it. I got a 90%. I was so happy to see my improvement, as it was really hard. Step by step I understood, and I knew it wouldn't be so bad after all.

"Science has always been my hardest subject area. But with a little positive effort and trying my hardest, I knew nothing was impossible."

My teacher, Ms. Edwards, responded with some very encouraging words I will not forget: "This is so positive. It does help to just keep working at something and not give up. But it's hard!"

My third grade teacher, Traci Brady Cormier, also

instilled a sense of hope in me. She made learning fun even when it was hard. Despite struggling in a few areas, she gave me the tools I needed to be successful. She invested in me as a student and made learning engaging to a student who was frustrated. Ms. Brady is one of the most cheerful, uplifting, and inspirational teachers I know. Coming to her class was inviting to a student, even one that didn't get the material right away. Her investment in me was what kept me doing my best, and her love for education and students made me want to become a teacher. Having her as a teacher, not only gave me hope, but it made me want to help others by providing the same hope she did for me. I am grateful that I learned under her, as her inspiration and drive like is none other. As a teacher, I want to be more like her.

It was teachers like my high school English teacher, Mrs. Edwards, who showed me that teaching is not necessarily about passing on information; it is instilling a passion for learning and the material. In my senior year I got very ill and was out of school for over a month. When I emailed her about trying to catch up, she encouraged me not to worry about it, but to focus on getting better. When I finally arrived at school, she even allowed me to take an oral test instead of a written one due to the stress and pressure of catching up. After many hours of tutor labs, I began to understand the material. She poured herself into her students and wanted to see them succeed. I love this about a teacher! Mrs. Edwards helped develop my 'voice' in writing, and encouraged me in my writing and in my love for reading. Even beyond high school, she helped me with papers in college, wanting to help me succeed. I am grateful for the ways she gave me hope.

It is teachers like these that gave me hope. Hope that I could understand concepts and hope that I would succeed if I put my mind to it.

Ever since these teachers began to instill a glimpse of hope in me, I wanted to do the same and give hope to others in their education, encouraging students that they can do it. I wanted to help them understand that they could be successful, that they could do anything they set their minds to, as Mrs. Blaubach taught me. I knew since third grade with Ms. Brady that I desired to become a teacher. It became even clearer to me when I got involved in Student Life in fourth grade. Helping around the school in this organization eventually led to three different deputy head positions during my high school years. I worked hard to help others around the school as so many people there had helped for me. I worked hard with the Student Life programs to develop and grow the program with the help of teachers and administrators. It gave me a sense of identity and purpose to help plan and execute events for the student body as a whole.

Some scholars say their 'home' is the classroom. For me, my home was the stage. Being a shy child, I wasn't the one who auditioned for solos or auditioned for major roles. Although I loved it, I was too shy to participate in featured roles. I started getting involved in my church's youth choir and musical. There I had my first speaking part. I was thrilled to have some lines! I thought this might be a good way to try performing a little and see if I really liked it.

My first starring appearance was at show choir camp in sixth grade. My best friend, Britany, asked me to come to camp with her. Her parents ran the camp, and I thought it would be fun to hang out with her. She kept telling me how exhilarating it would be. To my surprise, the camp triggered in me a love for performing. I loved being on stage! It gave me a place to have a voice when I was too shy to speak for myself.

Throughout middle school, I gained more and more confidence. Eventually I landed a solo in the eighth grade's show choir performance. I could not have been happier. I am grateful for Mrs. Colleen

Everitt: my teacher, role model, mentor, coach, and friend, for giving me that solo. Even though it was a short solo, it gave me confidence. It gave me hope that I could perform. Unlike many of my classmates, I had to overcome my shyness. Colleen helped me do that. I kept attending show choir camp. I auditioned for high school show choir and concert choir and got in! It was such an amazing feeling! I ended up being the cast captain in my senior year because of the diligence and drive that Colleen saw in me. For the past six years, I have been helping at the show choir camp, being everything from: an RA (resident assistant), a mom, a nurse, and an assistant choreographer, to the co-director of the drama elective.

Even though people who know me now would never guess that I was a shy child, I was. I needed to overcome my shyness. I needed something that would help me to be in front of people. Performing did that for me. Not only did performing help me to overcome my shyness, it became a passion of mine; it was a place that made me feel just like everyone else. It was a space where I could be me. It was a place that I could explore and not be graded on how well I did. It was a place that I realized I belonged. Classes were a challenge for me. The stage was a place that gave me freedom. I felt that my disabilities weren't affected by performing. In fact, I barely needed any accommodations. It was an area I could succeed in. It was a place that I didn't feel alone. I felt like others. When you have a medical condition that impacts your every being, being in a class or a place that you feel like your classmates is a major feeling. A feeling of acceptance. A place I belonged.

My experience in theatre and acting, though, was different. I loved music! When I was growing up, my parents took me to see many musicals, shows, and orchestra concerts. I started taking instrumental lessons, starting in the third grade playing piano and moving to violin in fourth grade. By middle school, I was playing violin in the high school orchestra and even played in the Greater Youth Twin Cities Symphony (GYTCS). In high school, I started taking guitar and voices lessons and have been passionate about guitar and voice ever since. I was passionate about music.

The first theater production I saw was *Joseph and the Amazing Technicolor Dreamcoat* with Donny Osmond at the Ordway when I was seven years old. I fell in love with musical theatre. Although it was something I loved seeing, I never thought in a million years I would actually do it.

In ninth grade, two of my close friends begged me to join drama. They insisted it would not only be fun for us to do together, but I would enjoy it. I fought it for a while and kept telling them it wasn't for me, when in reality, I was too shy. I didn't think I could do it or would even get cast. On the day of auditions, I decided to wander down to the performing arts area. I just thought I'd listen in on the auditions and cheer my friends on. Much to my surprise, Mrs. Everitt came out and encouraged me to read for a part. Saying why not, I auditioned, and got a role as Elaine in *Our Miss Brooks*. From there, I was hooked on theatre. I loved everything about being on stage, from the acting to the musical numbers. It gave me confidence. I was in *You Can't Take It with You* and *Our Town* my sophomore and senior years.

I loved the thrill and anticipation of being on stage. The stage gave me hope, as I spent many late nights there. My senior year I even took on an assistant director role, helping Mrs. Everitt direct the middle school show, *All I Really Need to Know I Learned in Kindergarten*. As I took my mark at the last concert choir show in 2005, I remembered where I came from and how I had to overcome my shyness. I remembered the fact that this was a place where I felt like others. Today, I am teaching students the joys and thrills of acting, singing, and dancing. I also perform in various theatre companies in town. It is my passion and what makes me tick.

Performing feels like home to me now. Even though I didn't necessarily want to perform or have the confidence to stand on stage when I was young, it gave me hope that I could use my body, voice, and imagination to create something beautiful. I had an excellent teacher who quickly became a mentor and coach. She invested her time and skills in me and helped me develop as a performer. Colleen instilled in me a deep sense of confidence and hope that I could do this. She developed my talent and saw me through my shyness.

Without her dedication to helping me succeed, I would not be where I am today. My teacher, whom I now call friend, helped show me that the stage is a 'home' and a safe place for me to express myself. It was her positivity that pushed me onto the stage. Her guidance, love for the arts, and love for me made me realize my potential. At the end of my senior year, she awarded me with the most improved drama award and saw something in me that I had never really seen in myself.

I have had many teachers throughout my life that have been positive, encouraging, and uplifting—too many in fact to write about here. However, I realize how grateful I am for each and every one of them providing me with a glimpse of positivity and hope.

When it came time to choose a college, I knew I wanted to attend a private, Christian, liberal arts school in the Midwest, preferably in either the Twin Cities area or Chicago. My first college visit was just thirty-five minutes away from my house, at Bethel University. I fell in love with the college and immediately knew that this was where I wanted to go to school. However, I continued to look at other colleges in the area and applied to many of them. When it came down to it, though, I wasn't sure if I would get in anywhere except maybe Normandale Community College. I had decent grades in high school and excellent teacher recommendations, yet very poor ACT scores. After taking the ACT numerous times and getting tutored for the ACT, I ended up with a score of 19. *What if I never get accepted into college?* The stress of getting into college was growing upon me. At this point, my self confidence in getting accepted to any college was lacking.

After sending in many applications between July and December 2004, I was accepted by three colleges, but one was on a provisional basis—Bethel University. The other two colleges welcomed me with open arms; one, in fact, gave me a scholarship. Bethel said I could attend, but only with a provisional status due to my low ACT scores. Despite my medically-challenging and sometimes near-death episodes, I managed to graduate from high school and get into Bethel University, the college of my choice.

Bethel has a great education department, which is one of the reasons I felt led there. It was a great fit for me, with a balance of academics, campus life, social activities, and faith. I felt 'at home' visiting the campus. Still, the provisionary status made me question whether I should attend another school. Was it worth attending the college of my dreams with provisionary status? After much prayer and consideration, I finalized my decision to attend Bethel University. I was excited for this new chapter in my life. After my first semester, I proved to Bethel that I was well-equipped and prepared for college and quickly was taken off probation.

I knew that my medical issues would require accommodations when attending college. I needed to be on the first floor of my dorm room so I wouldn't have to walk far. I needed a dorm that was close to classroom buildings and the cafeteria. I also needed to have a single room to accommodate my need for extra sleep. Having those accommodations made campus life much easier. By providing me with these, Bethel gave me the hope that college would be fine.

Bethel University was a 'well-fit' school for me. I got involved in many student programs and services, leading the multicultural programs and services, leading a choir as tour manager, and becoming president of the College Democrats. I had some amazing professors and staff members who truly cared about me and, my well-being, truly spurring me on like my 'ISM home.'

My greatest difficulties were in the education department. When I declared an education major, I struggled with some of the classes, including a math class I had to take twice, just like high school. It felt like I was in high school again, failing geometry. I always knew I wanted to be a teacher, but to keep failing core math and science classes was not encouraging. I knew teaching was what I was supposed to do. In fact, I have never had a job that didn't relate to teaching or working with kids. Several professors warned me that I would not make it as a teacher because I got sick so often.

Professors had their doubts about my teaching abilities due to my strength and stamina issues. I was heartbroken and devastated, as I knew that a teaching degree was my path. I could not see myself at the time doing anything different. I was determined and knew that nothing was going to stop me from reaching that dream. Unfortunately, due to extended sickness throughout college, I ended up needing to spend an extra semester in college. I am grateful to the Education Department at Bethel, though, for taking a chance on me, as I stand a proud teacher today.

Bethel gave me a great foundation for the real world, and I am grateful for my experiences there, especially the connections and education I received. With much diligence, determination, and drive, I graduated from Bethel University in December 2009. I even made the Dean's List one semester with an elementary education. Despite the challenges I had to overcome, I did it! I was overjoyed and excited to embark on a new adventure and new chapter of my life.

Chapter 8:
Plan B

"The Lord is close to the brokenhearted and saves those who are crushed in spirit." - Psalm 34:18

I was going to be an elementary school teacher. I got my B.A., passed my teaching license examinations, and by the end of January 2010, I was a licensed teacher. I was ready and excited for the next stage in life. Since I graduated in the middle of the school year, I began substitute teaching. It was busy spring and summer. I substitute taught in numerous schools, performed in a twenty-six show run of *The King and I*, taught summer school, and started to apply for full-time teaching jobs.

I spent my whole life preparing to be an elementary school teacher. Nearly every job on my resume was working with kids and teaching. I worked my whole life for this moment---to teach. It was my dream to teach. I wanted to help kids who struggled in school. Working with kids came natural to me and I loved everything about teaching. Despite the challenges, I already had overcome, I was ready to take on a classroom. To emulate my teacher and mentors that helped me. Little did I know that my life would soon be turned upside down!

I was going to be, I was, a teacher—until I got into a car accident. The car accident changed my life and set me on a totally new and different path. A path my planned and organized, type "A" personality was not ready for; one I didn't want. My car had been backed into with enough force to total it and I was left with injuries affecting many areas of my body. It led to a journey of healing and overcoming.

Shortly after the car accident, my body started behaving in ways it never had before. It was quite scary.

I had no idea at this time what was happening to me. All I knew was that something had triggered muscle spasms and pulling. My neck just wanted to go to the right. My shoulder crept up to my ear, and my pelvis was spasming so much it would throw me out of bed. Several times a week, I would wake up end up on the floor, due to the intense spasms. The contorted and twisted muscles made me literally see the world differently. Many times, I had to hold my neck to keep it still and at peace rather than shaking and moving all over the place. This is totally different from anything I had ever experienced before and left me writhing pain.

I looked weird and was in tremendous pain from the constant pulling. All I wanted was to be healed. People could literally see the pain in my face and body as my muscles tightened up. As my body pulled and contorted, my life changed. Doctors said that, because I was young and the condition was due to a post traumatic accident, I would heal more quickly than others. It has been over three years now. I am still healing. On top of mitochondria myopathy, on top of scoliosis, on top of visual-spatial disease, on top of asthma, I was soon to learn that I now suffered dystonia, a rare movement disorder. Can you say that again? Dis-tone-e-a? Dystonia? What is that? Is it a country? I never heard of it before. Think of it as similar to Parkinson's. The best way to describe it is an annoying kid constantly pulling your hair or pulling on your pant leg all day long. Constantly pulling, not letting go. Imagine how tiring that must be?

Dystonia reminds me of how the letters are shaped in this picture: contorted, twisted, and pulled to one side. Dystonia is a condition of your brain and muscles. It makes your body turn, twist, and move in uncontrollable ways. It is a devastating and life-changing condition, for which, sadly, there is no cure at this time. There are ways to mask the symptoms, but nothing to make it go away.

Let's go back to August, 2010, for a few moments. Close your eyes, take a deep breath, and imagine this is you. Here you are, a young, twenty-something college graduate, starting on your career, your lifelong dream. You have taught some this past spring, taught summer school, and completed a 26-show run of a musical. You are full of dreams, hopes, and aspirations for your life. You have the whole world ahead of you. Without warning, your life changes in the blink of your eye. You try to block out what has happened to realize that you just spent the last three years trying to cope and deal with your new life.

Now it is three years later...you now need to rest on a daily basis. You have tried several types of oral medication to see if anything helps; one is very addictive, but only helps a little. After more than two years, you have just begun to drive your car—only for short distances. You can only work a few hours here and there and are constantly tired from the muscles spasms. You lose friends and family, as they don't seem to understand what you are dealing with. You realize your dreams are gone, your car is gone, and you have no control over your body. You need to re-teach yourself how to do simple tasks such as eating, walking, and sleeping. You are in constant pain from the spasms, pulling, and twisting. Your life consists of more doctor appointments, Botox injections every couple of months, and physical therapy once a week. You are going through counseling to deal with the implications and learning to cope with this new way of life. You realize that you are in a vicious cycle of being constantly tired, yet trying to keep up and live a 'normal,' mid-twenty-year-old life.

Okay, how's the imagining going? I bet it is pretty hard to even begin to imagine this. As I write this, it is even hard for *me* to picture this happening. Well, this is reality for me. This is what happened to me. This is what I am learning to deal with on a daily basis, trying over and over again to comprehend the whole ordeal.

I remember that day. It is a day that I will probably never forget—a few days, to be exact. All I remember was sitting at my favorite Caribou Coffee a week after the car accident when I got the call.

The week after the car accident, the car insurance company gave me a rental car. I loved the car, and I was hopeful that they would be able to fix the little Saturn I was given for my 16th birthday. After a few days of driving the rental car, my dad got a phone call from the car dealer saying that my car was, in fact, totaled and they would not be able to fix it. I had to give it up. We didn't really have any other options but to let it go.

No, this can't be. This is *my* car. My car I drove for eight years or so. The car that I drove others around in. The car that I have many "car pictures" with my friends in. The car that many people knew, as I was known to shuttle friends both in high school and in college. I would have to give these memories up and get a new car. I didn't want a new car. I wasn't ready. It wasn't fair. I wasn't given any warning. I vividly recall my dad calling me while sitting at Caribou Coffee and asking me if I wanted to say goodbye to my car. I said "no," thinking it would be too hard to do so. I miss that car.

However, after much consideration, I purchased a Hyundai accent. It was a challenging decision, as I felt the pressure to buy a car right away and not stall on the decision-making process. It was such a rush decision. The Hyundai was a great car that sat in the garage for a few years as the dystonia progressed and I was unable to drive. Having it sit in the garage for years was a visual reminder to me of my sustained injury. Little did we know what was to come.

I remember that day: a day that I will not forget. It was a weekday about a week following the car accident. I was at home getting ready to see my chiropractor. My neck and pelvis began pulling, and I could barely focus on what I was doing as the pain settled in. As I held back the tears of the pain, I was determined to get to my appointment. Nothing was going to stop me. It was only a few miles down the road. *I can get there*, I thought. I was determined.

A few people suggested I should go to the doctor after the car accident. I was getting headaches, my body had spasms, and I had whiplash. So I made an appointment to see the chiropractor. I remember driving to the chiropractor's office about a week later. His office is only an eight-minute drive from my house. While I was driving to his office, I was in so much pain. I didn't want to go. I didn't have the energy to drive a few miles down the road.

The spasms were so intense, and my head was twisting so much, I thought it would literally fall off. I couldn't even see straight, with my neck and head tilted to the right—it jerked my whole body to the right. As I was driving, the spasms were so harsh that I pulled over on the side of the road twice on that eight-minute drive, so I could sit, rest, and breathe. My right foot had a difficult time getting from gas to brake quickly enough. I knew at this point, my life would be different, and I would have to give up many things I desired. I came into the doctor's office, fighting back the tears, fighting back my anger, sadness, and frustrations. What was I going to do? What were they going to do? I didn't want them to even touch me as my body was having so many spasms. I had lost the connection between my brain and my body. My brain told my body one thing, but my body did something else.

I somehow managed to get home that night. In the next few days, there were several moments when all I could do was bury my face in my pillow and cry. Cry, as I had lost hope. Cry, as my body was breaking. Cry, as I didn't know what to do next. Cry, as I had lost my dreams of teaching. Cry, as I spent much of my time in bed resting. Perhaps I was experiencing a similar feeling to failure to thrive as I did an infant. I spent a lot of time crying, trying to understand what was going on with my body, as my body had so many spasms. It felt like it wasn't my body. It was as though someone took it over. Many discouraged emotions came out during those days. The spasms, pulling, and twisting are still there, and when it is painful it puts me back in that day—where all I can do is cry. Losing control of your body is hard. I miss my body. I miss being able to do something without thinking about it. Now it takes every brain cell for me to accomplish each task.

At first, I didn't know what was going on with my body. The spasms, the tremors, the twisting, the pulling, and the pain were so intense. It was like my neck was twisting right off my body. After seeing a chiropractor for a few weeks, he recommended that I go to the University of Minnesota for a consultation for potential Botox injections. Botox? Isn't that for people who want to reduce wrinkles? Yes, it is for reducing wrinkles, but also for other types of medical issues. I was nervous, as I had no idea what to expect. I was ready to try everything and anything I could to help solve this weird, unrelenting problem.

I saw many other doctors before I found Dr. Dykstra. The chiropractor had a huge list of people that he wanted me to see. I spent many hours on the phone, trying make appointments and coordinate rides. I was so focused on healing and doing whatever I could to heal that I would see anyone and everyone that had some knowledge of dystonia and could potentially help me.

After a month, I was able to see Dr. Dennis Dykstra at the University of Minnesota. I talked with Tanya Baxter, Dr. Dykstra's assistant, to make sure I had everything I needed before this big appointment, an appointment that would help diagnose my problems and hopefully lead me to a path of healing. Dr. Dykstra (Dr. D) recommended that I get a CT scan of the C1 and C2 vertebrae (upper neck area). Another test? I had already gotten x-rays and MRIs a few weeks before from the chiropractor. Despite that, I walked down a long hallway to the CT room. The technicians asked me to lie down and hold still. My neck kept having spasms and jerking me all over, which made the CT scan very difficult. They managed to get a few good pictures, though, showing that the C1 and C2 vertebrate were displaced and twisted. This confirmed the diagnosis of dystonia. After one month of not knowing what was wrong with me, finally learning the diagnosis was a huge relief. It put a diagnosis, a name, to this mysterious condition.

After watching my body spasm and noting how it moved, Dr. D. suggested that they put Botox in the affected muscles to calm them down. Botox kills the nerves growing around the affected muscles. This paralyzes the muscles and makes the spasms (usually) less intense.

To be honest, I wasn't quite convinced of this at first; however, I wanted to give it try, as there has been so much success with it. We had to be very cautious at first, as we didn't know how the Botox would affect the myopathy. Slowly and slowly we added more and more Botox in various muscles. I felt a relief for the first time in over a month. The Botox is not a cure, but it calmed my muscles and nervous system, and over time I was able to gain more stamina. While I hope to not have to keep putting poison in my body, it helps (for now).

The visits to Dr. D.'s are always an adventure. A good adventure, but an adventure nonetheless. When I first get to the clinic, there are usually a few resident doctors since it is a university clinic. These doctors are training to become doctors similar to Dr. D. They ask me several questions and then ask me to just sit there. They begin to stare at me as if something is wrong with me. The residents watch my body patterns and movements. Sometimes they do tests, similar to those that I experienced as a kid. "Can you do this? How about do that?" They're seeing if the dystonia kicks in worse when I do certain motions. I don't mind having resident doctors assess me, as that is how they learn and I realize that being a teacher and student teaching. However, it is so challenging when they just sit there and stare at me. I feel so exposed, like being naked for everyone to see me at my worst.

Dr. Dykstra' office is one of the warmest and most welcoming environments. I feel comfortable there. He is a hilarious doctor and knows how to use humor with his patients. I never know if he is telling me the truth or not. After a treatment, he always gives me "toilet water; make sure to flush it three times." He wishes me 'good luck' and always asks if I am doing 'gooder.' My favorite part of the experience, though, is getting rich. What doctor pays you to come see him? I get a few cents every time I go there. I am probably up to $4 by now.

The actual injections are another story. The injections are not fun. I will say, though, that having such a great care team does help! It is basically about twenty shots all around my neck, head, shoulder, and right leg. To be honest, my body is fighting so hard that it is hard to tell how many shots I am actually getting. It could be five; it could be thirty. I am so 'out of it' that I never really count. The Botox is quite painful, being injected in small places around your body while you're constantly moving. After the Botox treatments, I always feel so tired and sleep for a few days. It truly takes a lot out you.

Dr. Dykstra describes my injection process as a wrestling match. It is kind of funny, because that is totally true. So, you know the joke how many people does it take to screw on a light bulb? Well, it is (kind of) that way for me. You see, my body is a moving target. It is having spasms, jerking, and pulling so much that it is like throwing darts and never knowing if you are going to get the bulls eyes or slightly over. It truly is a wrestling match. When the resident doctors are there, all four people, Dr. Dykstra, Tanya, and the two 'res docs,' all take part in it. Usually, Dr. D. finds the muscles and injects the needle into my body. Tanya holds me down and injects the Botox. One resident doctor holds me down and turns on the EMG machine. The other resident doctor reads off the various muscle groups and takes notes.

You may be wondering what an EMG machine is; The EMG machine is an amazing instrument to see where the affected muscles are. The doctors hook your body up to the machine through electrode stickers. They then put a tiny needle into the affected area of your body and turn on the EMG machine. When they find the right muscle, they turn the switch of the machine and it makes static noises, similar to those you get switching a radio station. The noises indicate if it is a bad muscle (pulling a lot) or if it is not pulling as much. It is truly an adventure, a wrestling match, and a game of darts all at the same time.

A bonus of injections is getting to know the amazing Tanya Baxter. Tanya is Dr. Dykstra's right-hand woman: 'the boss.' When am not sure if Dr. D. is telling the truth, she gives me the 'look.' This 'look' is a reminder to me that Dr. Dysktra is rarely telling the truth—but he is one of the smartest guys I know. Tanya is a Godsend to me. I don't know where I'd be without her. She makes the clinic the welcoming place it is. Tanya is always comforting, at every appointment, encouraging, and supportive. She goes the extra mile for me.

After my injections, she 'works on me' since she has a physical therapy background. She stays with me while I recovery from the injections, sharing life with me, and has become a great support and friend. There are times when I just need help. I need someone 'who gets it.' I know I can call Tanya at those times, for help, advice, and support. Even when the times are extra hard and I know that she is not in the office as it is later in the evening, I call her voicemail just to hear her voice as she is so encouraging for me.

After a month or so of the pulling, I felt there was something else that I could do. One of my best friends, Laurine, suggested I get in to see a physical therapist, Jill, who has lots of experience with treating dystonia. I said, "I'll do anything to make this better." It was a blessing to think, though, that if she'd helped my friend with dystonia, she might be able to help me as well. It gave me confidence and courage. I also knew Jill was a Christian, and I was thrilled to be able to work with someone who would pray for me as she worked hard to figure out the pattern of my body's movements and what to do with me. October 6th, 2010 was my first appointment with Jill. I have been seeing her once a week for the past three years or so.

Jill uses a special technique called mechanical link, which calms down the nervous system. Jill described mechanical link: "It differs from other techniques because it looks at the body as a whole, not merely as individual parts. As a result, the practitioner is better equipped to treat the client because they have the whole picture of how each of the body parts works together."

After every physical therapy session, I am exhausted. I eat a ton afterward and fall asleep for the rest of the day. The treatments are intense.

After seeing Jill practically weekly for now three years, she quickly became a friend, role model, mentor, and someone I could trust. She has been one of my greatest teachers—teaching me how to live my life from how to sit, walk, eat, write, and daily living needs. I shared my frustrations, my passions—my life—with Jill. My physical therapy sessions became not just physical therapy sessions, but life sessions. She encouraged me, inspired me, supported me, and helped me get through. Jill instilled hope in me on days when I couldn't see much light. When I came into the clinic feeling hopeless, she was there, giving me hope and pushing me on to success. Jill never gave up on me, even though it could have been really easy to do so. There were times when I would email Jill and just needed help and encouragement. She was there.

One day, she emailed me with a YouTube video of the song "Blessings" by Laura Story. The email said, "I pray your steps are firm with the Lord." I was so touched by this. This became my theme song over the past few years. I listened and prayed this song on a daily basis. Her stories have touched my heart. They show how she doesn't give up on her struggles and doesn't give up on me. Jill seems to always know exactly what to say or do. Often I walk away from a physical therapy session, of course feeling physically better, but also with something to think about. It helps me realize that it is okay; things will get better

Another aspect that I love about Jill is that she is constantly thinking about how to help me. There are times when she emails me and encourages me to try some things or encourages me to go off sugar and gluten. She helped me to learn how to sit, eat, and walk in ways that reduced my spasms. We realized my heart rate would increase with the spasms, so she found ways to adapt. She is always willing to think of new ways and new strategies.

After several years, Jill realized that the spasms reduced when I use my left hand instead of the right. I am right-handed. I have always written with my right hand, thrown a ball with my right hand, brushed my teeth with my right hand, and eaten with my right hand. You name it. It was my right hand. My left side? I don't do anything with my left side. Through her guidance, ideas, and support, I am learning to write with my left hand, throw a ball with my left hand, pick up things with my left hand—you name it. I even bought a pair of left-handed scissors. I am even finding new sensory tricks that are helping me live, such as putting my left hand up by my head to help the muscles to spasm less. Also, she had the idea of taping certain parts of my body with Kineso tape to help with sensory tricks to make the spasms less. This has been so helpful to help regain my life back to a 'new normal.'

Jill has truly been a blessing in my life, and I am so grateful for her. I truly believe that God put her in my life for a reason.

Dystonia does not give my muscles a break. They are constantly fighting 24/7. It is the fight or flight method. My body is in fight mode. My nervous system is wrecked and constantly firing. My doctor and physical therapist told me to rest and calm down my nervous system. My body was constantly moving/'running,' which is why they instructed me to sleep and rest. I hated this. This is not me. I am a 'type A', on the go, people person. You expect me to lie around at home and rest? I have to learn to deal with this new 'normal' and still am.

Chapter 9:
New Way to Live

"Beautiful Things" by Gungor, "This sickness is NOT until death, but for the glory of God that the son of God may be glorified in it." - John 11:4

The harder my body spasmed and the harder it fought, the more I lost sight of my dreams of teaching and performing. The more spasms I fought, the more my body worked in over time. At times, I literally lost my sight as I was typing on the computer and my neck and head would jerk to the right, causing me to not track the pages. Dealing with dystonia is not easy, and it has significantly altered my life. This was a whole new experience for me and my family. I had very little information on dystonia, and when I looked it up online, there was still little information to be found. I so desperately wanted to know more. The more information, the better. I spent many hours surfing the internet, desperately trying to find more about dystonia and movement disorders. Anything that would help me deal with the muscle spasms and involuntary movement; I was desperate.

Dystonia has been a constant battle. A battle of unrelenting pain, spasms, twitching, pulling, twisting, and contorting. It made my body move in incontrollable patterns. My legs even got into the whole scene and at times had spasms, pulling my whole body to the right. Walking became a challenge and every step I took was a challenge. Lying in bed with a spasming body is such a challenge.

It sucked a lot of energy from me. It took me so much effort to just get ready in the morning. Sometimes I wish that people would appreciate and understand the steps it took for me to even get there. Because of the constant pulling, I at times cancel coffee dates with people as I never know how I will be that day. It is different every day, let alone every hour of the day.

My body was having spasms and pulling so hard that all I wanted was a cure. I would do anything to find something that would heal me. I literally thought if I could get anyone who knows anything about dystonia's 'hands on me,' they might make me better. It seemed like I tried everything. I went to chiropractors, massage therapists, acupuncture, biofeedback, counseling, physical medicine, physical therapy, occupational therapy, a nutritionist—you name it—but they only seemed to help a little. My life consisted of doctor appointments. This time, though, the appointments were they weren't dreaded, as I wanted to do whatever it took. Tanya and Jill helped me to realize I had too many "cooks in the kitchen." I had to focus on a few core team players to help. They are: Dr. Dennis Dykstra, Tanya Baxter, and Jill: the best care team I could ask for.

Dystonia had left me bedridden for practically seven months. In between doctor's appoints, I slept, rested, and tried to relax my tight, spasming body. Being in bed for so long was hard for me. I missed my life. I missed my dreams. I missed my friends and family. I missed working as I thought I would be. My dreams were shattered, and all I could do was to lie in bed—sometimes it would be more like spasm in bed. I tried so hard to fight this off, as though it was a bad flu that would go away with sleep and rest. Every day I stayed in bed. It was horrible, lonely, and I don't ever want to be back there again. In many ways, I felt I'd lost 'everything.'

I had all the energy and yet very little energy. My energy was focused in the spasms, tossing me around, jerking and contorting me like rock singer Joe Cocker. At times, the spasms were so bad that they threw me out of bed, and I would end up on the floor. My body fought so hard it was in fight or flight mode, wanting to fight off anything that came its way. I was able to work a few small very part-time jobs, but as soon as I got home I would be back in bed, writhing in pain until I could see Jill again or get Botox injections. I spent little time seeing friends and much time in bed. This was depressing and hard for an extroverted, people person like me. How could this be happening to me?

Why was I left bedridden and ultimately heartbroken? Where was my life going?

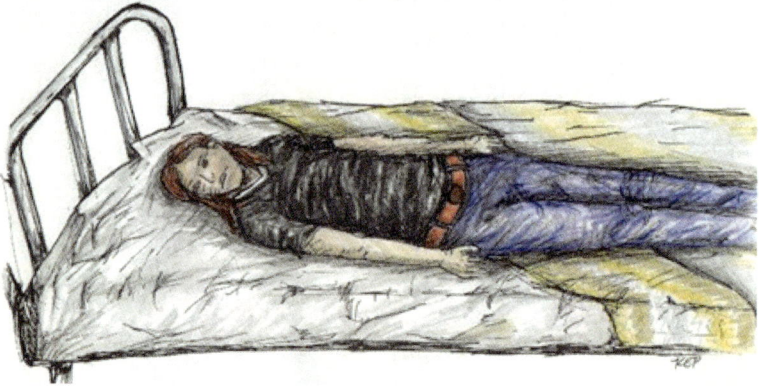

I felt as though I had lost everything: my work, my family, my friends, and my dreams. My dreams of becoming a teacher slowly vanished. My family didn't understand what I was going through. My friends and I were at a different page in life. Dystonia had my muscles pulling, twisting, and contorting. My brain told me to do one thing, and my body would do something else. I would try to eat, and I would miss my mouth. I had to reteach myself how to eat again. It was like my brain said one thing and did another. How annoying was that? Really? Come on. All I wanted was to be back to where I had control of my body and didn't have to think about every move I made. I lost my body. I grieved this loss.

I had so many spasms that it became a challenge to even type on the computer. The jerks pulled my head to the right, so it was hard to type, let alone sit. I was unable to drive, with the limited range of motion in my neck muscles. I missed driving. I missed my car. How was I supposed to get to appointments? To work? To see friends? I had to constantly rely on others for their help. I felt so hopeless. I was unable to work full time. I couldn't play my guitar for a year. Every time I tried to pick up my guitar, my neck would spasm more, and I was unable to see the music or where my fingers should go.

Driving was nearly impossible. In fact, I didn't drive a car for two and half years. I rode with metro mobility. Relying on others to pick me up and drop me off in a timely fashion was a nightmare. While I appreciate the service they have of getting anywhere you want to go in the Twin Cities for only $3 or $4 depending on the time of day, it became a pain trying to schedule it all and get to where I needed to be on time. Sometimes I sat on bus so long that it made the dystonia even worse. It made me want to give up. Why even use this service? I can just sit at home and not be bounced around in a noisy, hard-on-your-body bus.

I felt so alone, so desperate for a cure; for something that would heal me. I didn't get it. I needed something to keep me going. I could not believe what was happening: watching my friends find jobs or get married while I was at home unable to sleep, unable to do the simplest of tasks. It tore me to the core. It became worse as time went on. I could barely eat or do simple movements. Even walking was a struggle for me. I had trouble moving just a few feet. Taking a shower became nearly impossible, and I cried every time I stepped the shower, as the pain would settle in. I couldn't reach my head to wash my hair, and it often made the spasms worse. At times talking a shower is so hard, I am near tears every time. I struggled to sleep and sit. Sitting was the hardest for me, and I felt so embarrassed that I retreated. I didn't have much strength for anything.

I have always loved taking pictures of people and myself. Every time I took a picture of myself that year,

I looked at it and saw the pain in my face, the pain of my neck, and how twisted it looked. It made me so sad, and I didn't want to look at myself in those pictures, as it made me sad to see a person struggling, having spasms, and fighting so hard.

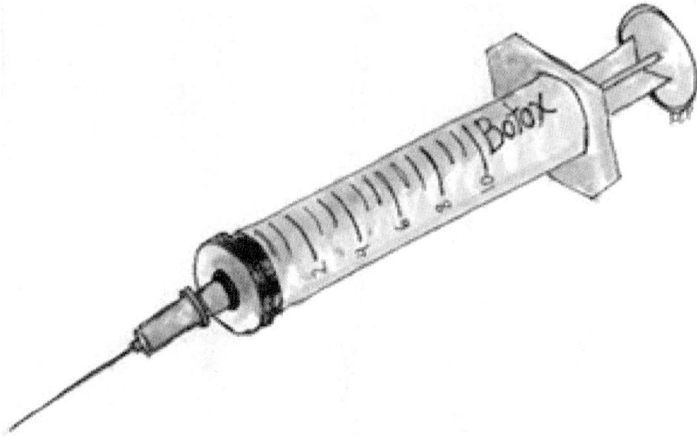

The Botox and physical therapy helped tremendously. Botox at times hurt my vocal chords, and my neck pulled so much that I couldn't do what I loved—singing and playing guitar. Dystonia had pulled my body in so many ways that I lost something I loved. I had taken three years of private guitar lessons in high school and had been playing ever since. I took countless voice lessons from elementary school through college. I missed that and longed for those days to return. Often I stared at my guitar in my room, wishing and hoping to play again. Sometimes I tried to pick it up and play a little, realizing that my body had even more spasms as I played. Its presence is a daily reminder that I am not the same person. It stared me back in the face. Often, it left me sad, distraught, and angry about this loss in my life. There were times when I just needed to put my guitar in the closet, so I wouldn't be tempted to try to play it or look at it. Looking at my guitar was just a constant reminder to me of my loss.

The initial period of my dystonia was the worst. I

had no idea what was going on with my body. To this day, it remains a mystery at times. I don't understand what is happening to my body. I see the world to the right with the spasms in my body pulling me to the right. Because my head, neck, and shoulder go the right, I have a skewed view of the world. I only see things to the right. At a restaurant, I have to choose where people sit and place them where I can see them. Don't be offended if I ask you to sit somewhere else or move so that I can see you. When my parents come into my room while I'm in bed and say, "Dinner's ready," I have to remind them and say, "I can't see you." This is so frustrating for me not to be able to see and have full range of motion in my neck.

A common theme over the past few years has been, "You look fine. You seem to be doing better. I don't see the spasms. You must be feeling better." I'm so tired of these comments. While I understand that I may 'look good,' it doesn't mean that I am not suffering on a daily basis. Then there are the weird stares as if something was wrong with me. Like what are you doing? Are you okay? As if I was having a seizure. People wonder what is wrong with me or wonder if I need to be taken to the emergency room. I am fine, my body just spasms and moves. I can't sit still. I often sit with my legs crossed and up to my chest to calm the spasms. I often come home distraught, because I am unable to be normal. People expect you to behave a certain way, but you can't when you have to sit in an unusual way to reduce spasms. I go to interviews, trying so hard to sit normally, when my legs just spasm all over the place. I often come home crying, as I am unable to sit normally. It reminds me of the 'look' that I got in regards to my race and skin color. It is hard to go into a full explanation of what dystonia is, since it is not well known.

I never know when the spasms are coming and how they will come. There are times when I get weird stares, as if something is wrong with me. Often I sit in an interview, formal meeting, a play, movie, or dinner, and the spasms get worse. People give me weird stares when this happens or when my head is tilted to the right and my shoulder has come up to my head. Often, I have to explain to people what is happening to my body. People just don't understand. I have become so self-conscious when my neck is tilted one way. It is frustrating to me. I don't want to feel this way. I have become less extroverted because of the pulling, spasms, and pain that happen. This is not me; I am not an introvert, although the constant pulling has given me more and more of a desire to stay at home rather than go out because it takes so much energy. Often, I find myself explaining to people what is happening to my body. People just don't understand.

Another aspect of the dystonia that has significantly impacted me has been my equilibrium, sense of direction, and balance. Since battling dystonia, I have fallen several times. I often feel as though the wall is attacking me; I run into it as though it is coming at me.

My life has changed in many ways. I used to work out at Lifetime Fitness, lifting weights and doing light cardio: walking, karate, and dance. Now I am limited in what I am able to physically do. Because I tire easily, household chores are a struggle. I am able to do a little here and there, but dystonia makes everything harder. If I wash dishes, that is all I have energy for. By the end of washing them, my body is having spasms and working even harder.

Overall, what has helped me? Besides physical therapy, Botox, and my amazing care team, it has to be the dystonia support group communities, both the ones that meet locally in the Twin Cities and the one on Facebook. Through them, I am able to connect with people who understand what I am going through and who are able to relate to me. This is truly huge for me. I get together with several support group members in person every few months and I am encouraged by their stories. They give me hope.

Another aspect that was huge in my growth, though, was through the lay care team at my church. A friend suggested that I talk with a lay care faith walker. I had no idea what that meant, but I thought it would be a good idea to meet with someone that could give me perspective, help me to have faith, pray for me, encourage me, and listen to me. Kyle Jackson, my youth pastor, had just the right person that would speak life into me. Marianne Milano had agreed to work with me. I was so thankful for that. She called me right around that Christmas, and we had our first meeting in January. I was still in so much pain at that time. I felt ashamed to ask her for rides, to help me run errands, or take me out for coffee. It turned out, though, that Marianne was truly a gift to me and I was a blessing to her. She mentored me and took me out on a weekly or semiweekly basis; some days it was to get me out of the house, some days it was to talk, some days it was just to have someone to talk to. I always knew Marianne would listen to my struggles and be there for me. When I didn't know where to turn, Marianne sent me notes of encouragements, emails, and text messages. Always at the exact moment I needed it, an email or coffee date would be awaiting me. We quickly became friends, and she continues to be an inspiration of hope to me. She saw hope for me when all I saw was darkness.

When something like this happens, we all go through stages of grief. I do still. In fact, I still get Botox injections every nine weeks, physical therapy once a week, medication daily, rest, and massages. My driving is limited. My work is also still limited, with a maximum of about a ten- to fifteen-hour week. I have realized every time I did something or tried to make it better, my body fought harder. I am healing, slowly. I am getting better. I am now able to play guitar. I am able to travel. I am able to sit longer. I am able to do so much more than before. I have come so far.

Still, sometimes just talking about the dystonia makes the dystonia pull harder.

People have told me that dystonia affects what you love the most. For me, it affects my whole life. What I loved was my life. I loved what I had and what I was hoping for. It was hard to realize that dystonia was attacking my body—and my brain. Dystonia affects your brain. I use my brain to think and teach in my job. It tried to steal my joy of teaching and my joy of life. Sometimes this makes life more challenging for me, as it attacks my brain and makes me move in uncontrollable ways. I don't want to let dystonia rob me of what I love.

"My God, my God, why have You forsaken me?"
I prayed daily that He would take away the pain, and
yet every day I writhed in pain, spasms, and pulling.
"If You're a loving God, why have You allowed this to
happen to me? What if my life was different? What if I
didn't have to go through these things? Why did You
choose me?" I already had enough burdens. I didn't
need yet another challenge.

There were times when I felt so alone. I felt like
no one understood what I was going through. I felt
as though I would talk to someone about it and they
didn't care or want to try to understand. People would
ask me how I was doing and if I was better, as though
it was the flu and I just needed a little time to get rid
of it. People asked me when I could drive again. I don't
know. I will let you know when I know, I seemed to
reply on a daily basis. No one understood my pain and
struggles. No one knew what to do with me. No one
understood the grief and loss that I endured. No one
understood the constant pulling and muscle spasms.
No one understood how foggy my brain felt. All I wanted was someone to listen to me and to be understood.
My friends were all out living their twenty-some-

thing lives, getting jobs, getting married, having kids; and here I was, lying in bed. I felt so isolated. It became harder for me to even relate to my friends. It was as though we were on a different playing field. They were playing chess while I was playing checkers. I felt like I had lost 'everything.' Why did I have to go through another physical hardship?

Many friends came in and out of my life during this time. I was so encouraged by the amazing people God put in my life. A close college roommate surprised me with a card that said, "Every plant that ever grew had to go through a whole lot of dirt to get there. I just wanted to send you a quick note of encouragement. I know you're dealing with a lot of hard things right now, but I know you know that your shining spirit and faith are such an encouragement to the rest of us. Love you." Another close friend from church wrote me a card saying, "Nikki, I've watched you walk with Jesus through this hard season since your accident with both grace and integrity. You've been honest about the pain and questions, but persevered, clinging to Jesus, taking it a day at a time. Never forget how deeply you are loved and cherished by God." It was people like these that made hope ring true a little louder.

I was blessed by a friend, who quickly became one of my best friends and a prayer warrior: Laurine. Laurine and I met through performing in a show together. Laurine showed me the path and guided me toward healing. Because she struggled with similar challenges, we were able to walk through this together. She took me by the hand and walked with me through this. Laurine gave me hope. She inspired me by her own struggles and life story. Laurine's faith showed through it all, despite the most challenging of times. I encouraged her, and she encouraged me. It was so amazing to find a friend who I could pray for and she would pray for me. I had the opportunity to take several trips with her to Europe to receive medical help from a physical therapist in Lille, France. Every time I said I couldn't do it, she took my hand, looked me in the eyes, and said, "I am here for you. You will get through this. One day you will be at the bedside of someone going through this helping them along." I would not be where I am today without her. Hope was all around me. I just needed to find it and believe in it.

Chapter 10:
Process, Learning, Reflections

"He's Always Been Faithful" - Sara Groves

I am overcoming life's challenges by looking at them as opportunities rather than as challenges. I see how my life can impact another person's life by the power of sharing my story. It would be easy to walk around as though there were a cloud over my head. Thinking unhopeful thoughts, as though life was horrible, and comparing myself to others. People often ask me, "How are you doing?" Do I say, "Oh I'm fine" (when really I'm struggling), or do I say, "I'm having spasms and pulling and am in pain"?

I can ignore my cultural identity or ignore my disabilities, but I choose to live in hope that it will be okay. I choose to embrace the whole me. I don't want to hide behind something or put on a mask without sharing my full story. I choose to live knowing that I can help others that are going through similar challenges. There are times when I wish I could change the past or how things happened. It doesn't do any good to dwell on the past but to be present and live in the here and now. God's will for our lives is more about the journey than the destination. I see hope in life; I see purpose and meaning in life. I want to make a difference in the lives of others in helping them see their potential, worth, and value as so many have for me.

I look at the sun and thank God for it. When I see the smile of a kid playing I see hope in it. I look at the flowers growing in the ground and realize how beautiful they are. I see the snow in the winter, and even though I am not a 'winter person,' I see that snow brings a change in seasons and a change in life, which brings about hope.

What have I learned? I have learned to ask for help. I can't do this all on my own. It is hard to ask for help. I want to do things myself and not be dependent on others. When I was bedridden, I needed to get to appointments and was unable to drive. What was I supposed to do? Both my parents worked, my brother was in school; how would I get to my doctor's appointments? Take a taxi cab and pay $100 for both ways? I don't think so. Eventually, I got the courage and strength to ask friends for help. Little did I know, they were more than willing to help me. My fear was that no one wanted to help, people were too busy, or didn't care. Yet, to my surprise, people were so gracious of their time, money, and support. I have been so used to giving and helping others, I didn't know how to ask for help or even to know what that looked like. I gave my life to people; asking for help was a lot harder than I thought.

I have learned to slow down. I had always been an 'on the go person,' running from activity to activity, burning the candle on both ends, leaving the house at 8:00 a.m. and returning at 10:00 p.m. I learned that it is okay to have a slower pace of life. This was a hard lesson to learn. I struggled with this for a while. I wanted to be on the go. I wanted to go and do something—anything I could. I didn't want to spend time at home by myself. Our society is such a fast-paced society that giving up 'always doing something' or seeing a friend was truly okay. It is okay to slow down, though, and is important to do so.

I have also learned to put my full trust, faith, and reliance in God. Before dystonia, I had a strong faith. Everyone saw that in me; it was obvious. I have learned to walk in that. Trust in God's love. Trust that He has a great and prosperous plan for me. I realize that my relationship with God is number one and He is what keeps me going and keeps me strong. Without God, I don't know where I'd be. He is able to do more than I could ever imagine or ask. I am alive today, and that is a true blue miracle.

I learned it is okay to grieve. I have gone through every stage of grief probably twice. It is okay to grieve. It is okay to grieve the loss of these things—my car, my body, my dreams. At first, I wanted to just shut it all away and act like it didn't really matter to me. I didn't realize that it was okay to be where I was at and acknowledge that where I am at is where I am. I am still grieving. It is a process. It is a challenge. It's hard to lose things that are so important to you—your body, your brain control, your dreams. I had huge dreams for my life, still do, but am realizing that it takes time when you lose things you love and are so important to you. It is okay to grieve.

I have learned that we all have our own battles to fight. My health challenges are my battle I am fighting. For some people, it is battling weight loss; for others, it is battling a divorce; for others, it is financial problems. There are many different problems that we all deal with and face. When we face our battles, it is easy for us to think, "Why me? Why do I have to go through this?" But it is important to acknowledge that we all have our own battles to face and mountains to climb. Each one of us.

I have also learned and accepted that I am physically, mentally, and emotionally about fifteen years older than I really am. Physically, they say that with all my medical problems, I have a body of a forty-year-old. Mentally and emotionally, I am not on the same level as many of the peers my age. I have gone through more life experiences than the average person. At times, it is hard for me to relate to those that are my age. I accept where I am. Even though it sucks at times and I'd much rather be where many of my peers are in their life stages, I am learning to accept where I am at.

I learned to live in the present. Being told as a young child that you would die in your teen years was life changing. I never really understood the impact of that on my life until much more recently. None of us know what tomorrow will bring. However, I cherish every day and every moment I get 'to be' because I never know how much more time I will have here on this earth.

I learned that it is important to hold on tight for dear life. None of us know what tomorrow will bring. We can't predict the future. What we can do is surround ourselves with God and people who will cheer us on and push us towards greatness.

I learned that we all have choices in life. Every day we make choices about what we will do, what we will wear, what we will eat, but ultimately it is how we live that is important. We can choose to be positive, or we can choose to be negative. I can say, "Gosh, I dislike being stuck at home needing to rest," or I can say what an incredible blessing it is to have opportunities to do other things. It is all our choice and how we look at things.

Finally, I learned there is much more to life than just getting a job, getting married, having kids, buying a house—living the 'American dream.' We all want to live the American dream. Many of us desire these things. I realized there is so much more to life than this. Yes, these are all important. Yes, I do want and still desire all of these marking, defining moments. Yet I also know there is so much more to life. Going through these experiences helped me to really appreciate every moment of life. I don't want to take anything for granted.

You see, I thought I'd be teaching in an elementary school. I thought I'd get a full-time teaching job, teaching fourth or fifth grade. I thought I would be making an impact in my students' lives in the classroom. This was not only my thoughts, but my hopes and dreams. I had high hopes. I always knew what I wanted to do. I went to school to become a full-time classroom teacher and filled my resume full of teaching and working with kids' experiences from the time I was in middle school. Sometimes we don't get to do what we want, desire, or plan. I thought teaching was my destiny.

Instead, I spend many days resting, taking two-hour afternoon naps, getting Botox injections, doing physical therapy, and practicing every day various tasks to regain my life. I work only part time to conserve energy and can drive only to places near my home. I'm not complaining, as I feel so blessed to be where I am and the progress I have made since then, but this was not what I thought I'd be doing.

It takes time. Time to grieve what you have lost. Time to start a new life. Time to regain a new way of living. It takes time to heal. To know what is right for your body. What to do. What not to do. Where to be. Where not to be. I am still learning this. I am learning to accept. To be. Life is hard, but it is how you look at it. I am not going to let dystonia or any other struggle take over my life.

Chapter 11:
My Hope

"Here I am! I stand at the door and knock. If anyone hears my voice and opens the door, I will come in and eat with that person and they with me."
- Revelation 3:20

149

My faith in God is number one. My philosophy is loving God and loving others. It wasn't always this way, though. In fact, it has been quite a journey for me to get to that place.

I grew up going to Christ Presbyterian Church in Edina, Minnesota nearly every Sunday with my parents. My parents brought me a children's Bible and other Christian books, music, and movies to help instigate my faith. I grew up singing "Jesus Loves Me" around the house, although not really knowing what that love really meant. I had all the defining moments in the Christian faith. I was baptized as an infant, got my first youth Bible in second grade, and took communion in elementary school. I didn't really believe in God, though. It was just 'something to do.' It wasn't my own faith. I believed, but it wasn't number one in my life.

As a child, I refused to go to Sunday school. There were a few reasons for this.

1. I didn't know many of the other children.

2. I was shy, extremely shy.

3. There were a lot of cliques in the church and I didn't feel like I belonged.

One thing my parents never did was force anything on me. When I wanted to go to church, I did and when I didn't, it was fine. As I mentioned, music was my passion and when I got a role in the fifth grade church musical I was elated. I figured I could belong there, singing and acting. The church didn't have many musical opportunities for middle school students, so I decided to not return to church. However, both God and my parents had different plans for me.

When I got into middle school, my parents encouraged me to return to church. They wanted me to go through commitment class in 8th grade and thought it would be helpful for me to meet people as I started middle school. I attended Online, which was the middle school youth program. The first year was super loud and crazy. Middle school students were wild. The staff had us play some crazy games and, being a shy kid, I often sat in the back and did my homework during the craziness of large group games. I had a great small group and an amazing small group leader who really invested in us. This is what kept me coming back week after week. After a year of Wednesday night programing, I wanted to learn more about who Jesus was, and I decided to go to the church's camp, Rockslide.

Asking my parents to go was another story. At first, they weren't too keen on me going with all my medical challenges. Rockslide was an outdoor, high-energy, physical activity camp. It was an amazing experience, though, that I will always remember. It was a truly mountain-top experience. You know those times when you realize there is a higher power—there is something out there? God was there and at that camp. I mean, God is everywhere, but God was truly at that camp. Words can't even begin to describe the experience I had there.

We packed up four school buses with our luggage and drove a few hours north to a camp in Wisconsin. Because I had several medical conditions, I could not do all the rock climbing, white river rafting, and all other the other outdoor activities. My parents were extremely nervous for me to go to this type of camp. While all the kids were out doing sports, my youth director, Brooks Wilkening, took the camp van and we drove to a nearby restaurant. It was a chance to learn, dig deep, connect, and understand. We ate lunch and talked about life. I asked her questions about God, and I could tell that God was real because Jesus kept shining through her. I am thankful for her taking the time to take me out to lunch and share her faith with me. I honestly thought I would be sitting in my cabin alone for a few hours while the others were enjoying the great outdoors. At first, I felt as though it wasn't fair. The other kids got to do all these fun activities and I was stuck back at the cabin. What Brooks did, though, was show me that God was real.

That night, the other youth director, Kyle Jackson, talked to us in a large group about how Jesus keeps knocking at our hearts and how important it is for us to become a part of His family and believe. He quoted the verse, "Here I am! I stand at the door and knock. If anyone hears my voice and opens the door, I will come in and eat with him and he with me" (Revelations 3:20). I remember his sermon being so dynamic, so convincing, and so engaging. Kyle's face lit up when he talked about God. It was so contagious. After this sermon, Kyle encouraged us to go into the woods by ourselves and pray the greatest prayer ever by asking Jesus to come into our lives. We all dispersed throughout the wooded lands to pray. I was so nervous as I'd never really prayed before. What do I say? How will He respond? I took a deep breath and prayed asking Jesus to come into my life. I admitted I was a sinner and I needed His love. I ran back to my cabin with my heart pounding and overflowing with the joy of our creator. My small group leader explained that I was now a part of God's family. I told this to Brooks and Kyle the next day, and they were excited I'd committed my life to Him. My faith grew and grew from there.

In seventh grade, I created my own Bible study with some friends at school. We decided to take our free period and find a room to do a Bible study. It was amazing to find other believers at school and have confidence in talking about it. Life didn't really change, though. I was not living a life that God would want me to. I didn't attend Wednesday night small groups as I thought church was all about asking Jesus into your heart, so I didn't feel I needed to go.

Eighth grade was commitment class. I was excited. I heard great things about what we would learn, do, and discuss. This was a powerful year—a life-changing year. Katie was my youth director. She often took me out for lunch or dinner to talk about my faith and invest in me. I could see by her faith it wasn't just asking Him to come into your life. It was a commitment and a daily living choice. I am so grateful for Katie's leadership that year. It made me who I am.

That April, I went on a retreat for commitment class. I had no idea what to expect on that retreat. The second night at the retreat we were lead to a dark room. Waiting in that dark room were all our leaders. They washed our feet, led us in communion, led us in worship, prayed over us, and shared stories with us. We talked about how our faith had grown. Our parents wrote us letters of how proud they were in taking this huge step. As we all read our letters and heard people's stories and our leader's prayers, streams of tears ran down our faces, tears of joy and of hope. This was the hope I had been looking for. This was the hope I was looking for as I was in the ER, waiting to hear back about medical tests or having ignorant comments about my race thrown at me.

My leader prayed this prayer: "Dear Lord, I thank You for Nikki. Her hunger and thirst for You is absolutely amazing to me. Her knowledge of Your word is such an inspiration. I pray that she continues to shine for You. Her quietness and big heart are such a special part to this group and I thank You for that." (At that time, I was extremely quiet, and didn't speak up much.) This prayer really stuck with me. It was a defining factor in building up my hope. It gave me hope that she believed in me and saw so many positive aspects about myself. Ever since then, I knew my faith in the Lord was important to me.

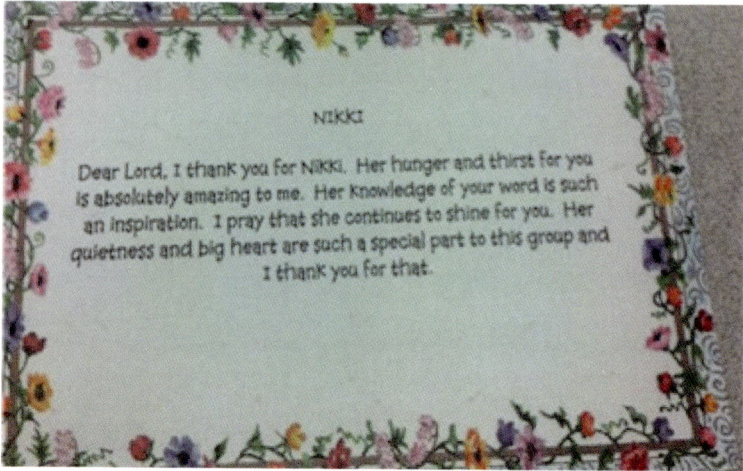

NIKKI

Dear Lord, I thank you for Nikki. Her hunger and thirst for you is absolutely amazing to me. Her knowledge of your word is such an inspiration. I pray that she continues to shine for you. Her quietness and big heart are such a special part to this group and I thank you for that.

That spring, I applied for leadership in the church to lead kids. I knew I wanted to work with kids and wanted to share this light that I now found with them. I have taught fourth and fifth graders for eight consecutive years at church all throughout high school and college. It amazes me as my students I lead are now in their first year out of college to sophomores in high school. I teach and lead students in faith through coaching. I try to follow God through the verse, "Let your light shine before all men, so they may see your good deeds and praise your Father in Heaven" (Matthew 5:16). This hope in Christ is so strong, and I have been so involved in taking the next steps in my faith to fully trust and lean on Him. There are times when I struggle and doubt, but I know that ultimately He is in control and loves us.

Throughout my teaching at church, there were many mentors that came into my life and encouraged me in my faith. I am grateful for each of them. Laura Mulliken was one of those mentors and leaders. Laura was my supervisor when I led in the kids' ministry. She quickly became a close friend, mentor, role model, leader, and supporter. I could always go to her for prayer, words of advice, wisdom, and guidance. We had many coffee dates where she poured life into me. Laura gave me a glimpse of hope. She encouraged me and always gave me exactly what I needed to hear. We still get together for coffee and at times worship together. I am grateful for being able to grow together with Laura. She continues to be an inspiration to me. Asking me the hard questions of life, encouraging me in what I do, and always asking me how I have seen God at work. Sometimes, I think Laura knew me better than I knew myself. She always was investing in me, in my life, and in my faith.

In many ways, she brought me up to the woman of God I am today. It has been neat to see the growth we had in our friendship. My senior year of high school, she sent me a card in the mail that read: "You hold a special place in my heart and in this world, and that makes you irreplaceable. It has been a joy and blessing to have you in my life these past years. I can't wait to see what God is going to do with your life these next years of college. Thank you for your devotion and preparation. You are amazing. Love, Laura." Laura gave me hope and faith that I am extremely grateful for.

I feel blessed for the relationships I have developed and those that have poured into me through CPC, as well as the Upper Room Community. I grew in my faith and learned that my hope is in Christ and in Christ alone.

Chapter 12:
Now What?

"Dare you to Move" - Switchfoot

In that darkest night of my soul, there was still a glimmer of a light at the end of the tunnel. That small glimpse, that small glimmer, was a glimpse of hope. I found a light because people had faith in *me*. They poured their life into me.

As I lay in bed, faces flashed before me of people who poured life into me. They told me that they believed in me, that there was hope, and that I could be a testimony to others.

Friends from church, friends from theatre,

friends from school, and friends from various walks of life stood shoulder to shoulder with me, cheering me on, picking me up when I fell, and saying they believed in me. They prayed for me, encouraged me, inspired me, and pushed me on, helping me to see when I couldn't. I knew that, even when I couldn't do much, I could help others by encouraging them. By encouraging them and giving them strength, they in turn gave me strength. They helped me realize all the incredible blessings in my life. I realized how grateful I was to be here and how my story might just impact one person.

It is not easy to have hope. I have had plenty of reasons not to have it. Yet I choose to have hope. Struggles, challenges, and obstacles were just a part of my life. They don't define who I am. I am thankful for them, as they inspired me to press on. That is what makes me who I am today: a go-getter, an achiever, a fighter, and an overcomer.

Having hope in something greater than myself.

Having hope to make a difference in this world.

Having hope that my story and my struggles will one day touch someone's life.

Having hope that God would heal me.

Having hope that we would find a cure for the various conditions I deal with on a daily basis and those that others deal with.

Having hope that people will unify as one and understand racial identity and adoption-related issues.

It is an everyday battle to choose hope; to walk another step, another day. I am grateful for every day I am given to help others overcome, to encourage others, and to be a light to others.

I might not have been able to do the simplest of tasks, but I had to if I was going to regain my life. I had to do something. I had learned to be a teacher. I would teach myself—how to walk, how to eat, how to sit, and how to do every day, normal things again. I would do it. I did do it. I am still doing it. I am still adjusting to a new way of life (for now). I am still healing.

You see, I went from no light, to a candle burning in the wind, to a fiery, burning bush. It was people, music, musicals, and books that kept me going. It was ultimately God that gave me hope. When I was bedridden, I looked up one day and said, "All I have and all I ever need is God." I knew that God was not finished with me yet.

In the beginning, I failed to thrive. I was given a slug of a scar upon my arm, and I was told I would only live to my early teens. The doctors didn't know how to "fix me." *Only Jesus knew how to fix me.* I had some doctors tell me they would not take me as their patient. My case frightened them.

I have to fight every day for understanding from others around me.

And yet, here I am, in my twenties and still alive! A walking, living, breathing testimony of the great work of God and what the power of positivity and hope can do in someone's life.

I am a proud martial artist in karate and a musical theatre dancer.

I graduated from college with a 3.16 GPA and was on the Dean's List. I have even taken graduate courses.

I am a proud teacher and teaching artist, passing to others the gifts of acting and dance.

I am a proud Korean adoptee, speaking up and encouraging other adoptees to share their stories, pain, struggles, and joys.

I am a creative person and use various outlets to

show others God's greatness through performing.

I view my disabilities as my ability to help someone else. I can help others through my compassion, seeing the good and positive aspects in people. My greatest desire is to help just one person in their life—then my job is done. To bring a smile to someone's face is what I long for, knowing that I have made a difference in the world.

All my life, struggles have made me the person I am today...a strong woman of faith who believes that I can do whatever I set my mind to. Because, you see, in the midst of pain and despair, I looked up and realized that all I have, all I need, and all I want is God.

I see the world differently. I see how to overcome. I see how to help others do the same.

I want to help others do the same—to overcome.

Growing up, I faced many obstacles. I learned to overcome each and every one of them. I am here to tell you, you can, too.

I know what it's like to not be 'like everyone else,' to want to 'fit in'—to be 'normal'—or to struggle with people thinking you are fine. I know how easy it is to lose hope. Yet, I choose hope. Hope that there will be another day, that God can make good come out of the bad.

I choose not to focus on the can'ts but to focus instead on the cans. What can I do? I could find the light in others. I could find the light within myself. I am here to share it with you.

Choose hope. Hope was at my fingertips; I had to reach out and grab it. I have to make a conscious effort to choose hope daily.

Boundaries merely help us find our true potential. All this I live with, and I am here to say, I live with hope. I choose to have hope.

We all do.

We all must.

I'm not here for your pity. I'm here to show you *your* potential. If I can do it, so can you. While I fight my medical challenges and my search for identity, I find *value* in who I am.

I am a fighter. I am an *overcomer*. It took me a while, however now I embrace my Korean American name—my identity.

I am a 'bright, shining, good-natured and victorious one'—Nikki Min Yeong.

Chapter 13:
Renew Hope

"Keep Holding On" - Avril Lavigne

It came to me in a dream. It was as though I was destined to do this. I was destined to inspire, empower, and motivate others on their life journey. Many people encouraged me by saying, "You are so positive about everything? How do you do it? If only there were more people like you." I heard comments like this most of my life. This is what spurred on the message and idea of hope.

After much prayer and consideration, I entitled this book *I Choose Hope.* Why? Because as much as this book is a memoir about my struggles and challenges, it is also about choosing hope. We choose many things in life. Let's think about it for a minute. When we get up in the morning, we choose whether or not we will eat breakfast and, if we eat breakfast, what will we eat. We choose what clothes we will wear. We choose what we will order and eat at lunch. Sometimes we don't have control over our choices. We can't choose the traffic lights making us late to work or school. We can't choose how our friends will respond to what we say or do. We can only make choices for ourselves.

I believe wholeheartedly that one choice we need to and should choose is hope. You might have a huge financial burden to deal with, a loved one who is dealing with cancer, or you might be in the middle of a divorce. Those are all not easy things to deal with and go through. However, we can choose our attitude towards them. We can say, "This sucks," and go into a depression because life is now horrible and everything is going wrong. Or we can choose hope, positivity, and believing that good will come out of it.

What is hope? What do you have hope in and hope for? Why do we need to have hope? Why choose hope? Hope is what we need. We need hope to survive, to live, and to be. We all need hope. Hope for things to get better. Hope for surviving life's challenges. Hope gives us direction. Hope gives us courage. How many people do you know that seem to live a hopeless life? How many of those people are happy about their lives and situations? Not very many, I suppose. Hope is a choice. It is how we live our lives. Struggles are a part of life. We can go through them with a cloud over our heads, or we can look at them as an opportunity. I think you can probably guess how I have come to live life...with HOPE!

Hope is like a scale where you weigh two objects. So let's say on one side of the scale there are so many hardships and obstacles to battle and the other side is this idea of hope. Even though the scale would probably tip more towards the challenges of life, hope always and will always outweigh it all.

What do we need to have hope? We need people. We need people around us to encourage us, to empower us, and to spur us on in life. Without people and ultimately without God, where is hope found?

Take a moment to chew on some food for thought. Discuss it with a friend over a cup of coffee. How can you change your attitude and outlook with hope?

1. *We are who we are. We can't change that.* I will always be a Korean American adoptee. I will always have a complex medical history. Even if I wanted to change my appearance or my abilities, I am who I am. You are who you are. *Accept where you are now.* The greatest aspect I am learning these days to do and be is to accept. Accept where I am at today. I can't change that.

2. *We can't change the past.* We need to learn from the past, stay in the present, and look to the future. Embrace who you are; embrace the incredible gifts and talents you bring to the world. You have unique gifts that only you can bring. Use them.

3. *Know your personality, who you are, and how*

you are wired. In the Myers-Briggs test, I am an ENTJ. I am an extrovert, intuitive, a thinker, and a judger. I am energized by the outside world, look for opportunities and connections, base my decisions on analysis, and am a planner. I am a lion and an otter in the behavior style. I like to control things, am results driven, and love the big picture of ideas. From the Strengths Finder, I am an achiever and activator, and have belief, focus, and individualization strengths. From the STRONG assessment, I am a social, enterprising, artistic person. I have shepherding, leadership, administration, and prophecy gifts. My personality is that of a choleric sanguine, which means I am a natural leader, energetic, determined, capable, and strong willed. *What are your gifts, talents, and abilities? How do you learn best? How are you using your wiring for the best? Take assessments, know who you are, and use your gifts and talents.* I encourage you to step into that. Take a look at what you're good at. Lean into those gifts. You have so much potential and so many gifts and talents to offer this world. Take it all in. *Do what you were created to do.*

4.   *Never Give Up!* In Jason Mraz's song "I Won't Give Up," he writes that we must not give up. Don't ever lose hope and give up on yourself, your dreams, or your aspirations in life.

5.   A friend once told me, "Be the best Nikki you can be. We can't ask for anything more." I challenge you, *be the best _____ (insert your name) you can be.* I can't be you; I can't even pretend to be. I can be, though, the best Nikki I know how to be. I can be the best person I know how to be. After all, I am not going to be anyone or anything but me. God made us each with a unique

set of gifts and talents. If we try to be anything but ourselves, we are selling ourselves short, and that is not what we are intended to do.

6. *When all else crumbles, you have faith.* We need to have faith in what we believe in and faith in who we are. We need something greater than ourselves.

7. *We all have choices in this life.* We have a choice of what we are going to wear. We have a choice of what coffee shop we go to. We have life-changing choices as well, such as what college we go to and what we major in. We can choose hope, or we can choose despair. *What are you going to choose?*

8. *Stay positive! Keep a positive outlook on life.* It is all about perspective. Always look on the bright side of life.

9. *Be thankful.* I am thankful to be adopted. I am even thankful for living with disabilities. I feel blessed to be where I am today.

10. *Be open.* I had a plan for my life. I planned to be an elementary school teacher. I planned and hoped to keep substitute teaching, teaching in various venues, and to land a classroom position. I had a plan. I thought I was in control of my life. Be open. Be open to wherever you are led to.

11. As you see throughout my story, I have had a plethora of mentors in my life. All of whom I want to highlight, give spotlight to. Thank you, I am grateful for each of you. Do you have a mentor? Are they investing in you? Are you investing in them? *Find a mentor. See how a mentor will change your life.*

12. As my high school science teacher and friend,

Amy Blaubach, says, "*You can do anything you set your mind to do.*" You can do it! You can change the world! Make a difference in the life of one person. When I student taught at a school called Creek Valley Elementary in Edina, MN, they had a motto that said, "Go MAD." At first I thought, *What is that? MAD?* I soon found out it stood for Go Out and Make a Difference. Believe you can make a difference.

13. I love playing cards. Life is like playing cards. We don't know what cards we will get, and we can't change the cards we are given. What can we do? We can only live with what we have. We can choose how to play our cards. You might get a 'bad hand' of cards. Do you think to yourself, "Oh, great; I have horrible cards," or do you say to yourself, "How can I use the cards I have to the best of my ability?" *My challenge to you is to use the cards to the best of your ability. You may have gotten a 'bad hand,' but what are you going to do with it?*

14. *What is your ultimate purpose? What is your goal? Why are you here? Know your goals. Why were you put on this earth? You are here for a reason. Find it, grab a hold of it, and work with it.*

Out of this idea of hope came my business, Renew Hope, LLC. Choosing hope is an everyday battle and choice. It is not a one-time decision. We need to constantly and consistently be choosing hope. It is a choice we need to make—which is why I started Renew Hope. The idea of Renew Hope is to empower, inspire, and motivate others on their journey. I wanted to give a voice to those that don't have one. I desire to help others to live their life to the fullest. Renew Hope, LLC came out of a dream. A dream in which people believed in me and encouraged me. The message is that when the whole world crumbles around you, there is still hope inside you, and it is essential for you to let it shine.

RenewHope!

So, what does hope stand for? I have come up with a core message for hope, and it is my desire for you to live by. You see, I was bedridden for seven months. What was I going to do with my life? How was I going to live? How was I going to contribute to society? This is when I came up with my core message and the theme to my life, as I rested in bed for days upon days. If you walk away with nothing else from this book, walk away with this idea of hope. H. O. P. E.

H-Hold on to Faith

Most of us have faith in something. What do you have faith in? Perhaps it is faith in God. Maybe it is faith in yourself. Do you have faith in others, your job, or a relationship? Maybe it is faith that you can do it. It is essential that we hold on to our faith and never lose it. When all else crumbles, we still have our faith and our beliefs. We need to hold on to our faith in whatever way that may be. Hold on to your faith. Grasp it. Capture it and seize it, and don't let it go. We need our faith. Hold on to whatever it is that keeps you going.

O-Opportunities

Look for opportunities. My lay care mentor, Marianne, encouraged me to look at all the things I could do. What can you do? I looked at all the opportunities that were out there that I could take part in. I thought to myself, I don't have the energy or stamina to do what I wanted to do, so what can I do instead? How could I be an encouragement to others? While I couldn't do a lot of things, I still had my voice; I could talk on the phone and encourage people that way. I still had the use of my hands; I could write emails to people. What can you do? Maybe you aren't able to do everything you did when you were young. Maybe you don't have money to do certain activities. What do you have, though? Look for opportunities where you can give back. When you give back to others, it makes you feel better. Look for opportunities. What can you do?

P-Process Learning

Reflect! I have talked about the power of journaling several times throughout this book. It is always important to process what we are learning. What are you learning through this trial or challenge? What can you learn from it? When I first got the news of dystonia, I hated it. I did everything I could do to get rid of it. I tried several types of medication, therapies, and other ways to heal myself. However, what was I learning from it all? I learned to slow down my life. I realized that my body could not handle what it used to handle. I learned I could not burn the candle on both ends. I learned to take time to reflect. Process what you are learning. What are you learning from your experience? What did I learn from my adoption? I learned people can be ignorant. Family is family and I am grateful for mine. It doesn't matter where you came from. Embrace who you are and the gifts you are given. What do you need to learn from your trials and obstacles? Take time to process what you're learning.

E-Encourage the Soul

Sometimes it is important to put yourself first.

Many times, we don't to do that. We live in a society that encourages us to give to others first. We put ourselves last. We give ourselves the leftovers. Here's the challenge: When you are in a situation of challenges, obstacles, and hurdles, what do you do? Take time to do something that encourages your soul. What are you doing to encourage your soul?

When I was lying in bed, I realized that I needed to take time for me. I took time to listen to music, read books, see movies, and sometimes go out with friends and go see shows and musicals. I did what I could do to make myself happy. When I saw a show, it took me away from my pain and trials and put me in a place where I could focus on something else. It is important to encourage our souls. Don't always focus on the trials. Take your mind off them for a while. Do something that encourages you. Being a performer, I try to see some type of play or musical once every few months; this encourages my soul. What are you doing to encourage yours?

So, who are you? Where can you find hope? You can find hope by first getting a journal. Journal and write down your experiences. Write down your greatest life lessons, your joys, struggles, fears, and passions. Accept yourself for who you are. Know that you are amazing and have so many gifts to offer this world. Trust yourself. Be the best you can be. Take it one day at a time. Remember, it is about the journey, not the destination. Find hope within yourself. Find hope around you. Choose hope.

Remember H. O. P. E:

H-Hold on to faith
O-Opportunities
P-Process Learning
E-Encourage the Soul

Chapter 14:
Writing Your Blueprint

"Be the change you wish to see in the world."
- Ghandi

Now it is your turn to write your story. Are there areas in your life that you need to overcome? What does it mean to overcome? How do you choose to live life? Living and appreciating life looks different for each of us. I know that for me, there have been times I have taken life for granted. I did not realize how short life truly is. I did not take time to smell the freshly cut flowers at the local market, or appreciate the person holding the Caribou Coffee door as I entered or the barista that gave an extra shot of chocolate in my mocha on a cold winter morning. Upon being diagnoses with dystonia, I discovered how precious life is. Too often we live in the past, are not fully present, and worry about the future. How are you living your life? Are you worried about what tomorrow will bring, or are you living in the moment? Do you appreciate life every minute of the day?

Having several near-death experiences, I learned that we aren't guaranteed anything. In fact, it has pushed me to be in the present. If someone told you that you had ten years to live, how would you live? This is how my life was like. I was told I would have ten more years to live at the age of six. Because of this, I try my best to be in the moment, as we don't know what tomorrow will bring. None of us do.

Think for a moment what it would be like if you only had a certain amount of days to live. How would you live? Are you living that way? If not, change the way you live to the way you want to become.

When I was bedridden, all I had was myself—and God. I had to be my own advocate. I learned that my life may not be like most people's, and I had to accept that despite how challenging it was. I may not have started a full-time job after college like so many of my peers, or experienced the typical milestones some have, but God had a different plan in store for me and I am thankful for it.

One of my favorite plays is *Our Town* by Thorton

Wilder. The protagonist, Emily Gibbs, asks the stage manager, "Do any human beings ever realize life while they live it—every, every minute? No—Saints and poets maybe—they do so." This is a perfect example of how we should live. Read the play. It gives an excellent example of how we should live, by realizing that the everyday things in life count and matter.

It was a huge process and endeavor to write a memoir of my life story. It took many hours with my computer, my thoughts and prayers, and reflections to be open, honest, real, and share my life with you. It is not an easy task. I knew, though, that I needed to share my story. I want to encourage you to write yours.

Architects have a blueprint for the buildings they construct. People who drive for a living have a map of where they are going to go. Teachers create lesson plans and instructional goals for their students. Many professions have blueprints, roadmaps, and goals. What is your blueprint for life? How do you want to be remembered? As someone who walks around with a cloud over their head, thinking about all the horrible things happening to them, or as a person that chooses life—as a person that chooses hope?

Hope is all around us! We need to look for it, grab a hold of it, and not let it go. We need to feel what hope feels like so when we lose hope we can grab it again. We need people around us to encourage us when we can't seem to find our way. If we all continued to press on and be hopeful, we would live a much more productive and happier life.

If you died today, what would you want people to say about you? Writing this memoir came out of people saying how positive and hopeful I was and how they really admired those qualities. This is an excellent example of how I want to live. So many people have said to me, "I really admire how hopeful you are. How inspiring you are. How you don't give up. How you have strength when it seems like life is hard. You have such a strength about you." To this, I say that it is all about hope. Having hope in God. Having hope that if my story can make a difference in one person's life, my job is done. I am grateful for that.

My motto in life is, "You can change the world." Since high school, I have had a framed poster in my bedroom that is a reminder of this phrase. If my story, my words, my love can affect just one person, one person's life, I am satisfied. What about you? What is your motto in life? How do you live your life? Know that the greatest thing we can have is hope and love. Your story *can* impact others.

Go! Grab a piece of paper, a pen, or your computer, and write your blueprint for life. How are you living your life? Share your story. The world needs more good stories. Always remember to remain hopeful and stay positive. Choose to live a hopeful life.

Best wishes on your own journey, and remember, always stay hopeful!

Staying hopeful,
Nikki Min Yeong Abramson

P.S. I would love to hear from you. What is your story? How did this book change you? What will you do now that you have read this book? Email me at nikki@nikkiabramson.com; I'd love to hear your story.

Caring Bridge Journal Entries

After a month and half of writhing in pain, I decided to start a caringbridge site. I posted my first journal entry on October 18, 2010, almost two months after dystonia started. I decided to use the website caringbridge.org to help bridge the gap between my family and friends in what was going on with my health. I am so grateful for caringbridge as it has given me space to journal and write updates on how I am doing. I had friends that used a caringbridge site, yet, I didn't ever think it would be me. Never in my wildest dreams would I write in a caringbrige site, unless I had an ill family member or something like that. It was a way to communicate and for this I am grateful for caringbridge.org to allow me to share my story.

Here are some of the journal entries. Read what you would like and journey with me through this challenging period of time.

October 18, 2010-Today was difficult...but praise God for rest! I am learning what it means to rest and relax. I am a type "A" person... a person that is constantly on the go! This is one of the hardest things for me to go through, to know what it means to REST... to not do anything...to not be consumed with life... I am always thinking I should be doing something...having this makes life difficult. I feel so helpless and unable to do much! It is not fun. I am praying that I can learn what it means to REST that I can heal and learn how to heal.

October 19, 2010-Yesterday, I had physical therapy and boy was it painful. Jill, my PT, says that my body is in fight mode of the idea fight or flight. My whole nervous system is on overload and is constantly going. The whole body was spasming, spasming so hard that it made her job difficult. I have been running around to all these doctors and appointments trying to heal quickly and throwing at my body everything I can think of when I am learning that I just need to slow down. There is no easy way out. There is no time-line for this. Doctors do not know if it will be a week, a month, or a year. The most difficult part of this is to realize that it will take time and I need to be patient. Having to rely on others to drive me places though is a challenge. At this point, I can't do any exercises yet. She also found out how weak my left side is. I can twist my foot on my right side and move my leg with no problem, however on the left side I can barely move it and have to use all my energy to do so.

Here's a helpful website in case you would like more information on what dystonia is:

www.spasmodictorticollis.org

What did the doctors say? It will take time...pa-tience...not sure how long it will take... my body espe-cially nervous system is bad... Please pray for peace to my body especially my nervous system.

October 20, 2010-Last night was difficult to sleep, no good position to be in...very painful.

October 21, 2010-Spasms are so bad...yester-day I thought the Botox was helping...help!

Yesterday, I went to see Dr. Dykstra at the U of M. He gave me more Botox injections in my neck. Bo-tox for those of you that don't know basically kills the nerve that is spasming. It makes the muscles less tense and makes the spasms cease. The Botox helps reduce spasms and calms the muscles down. My neck was really spasming hard. It is an interesting process. They hook you up to a machine with electrodes that use radio waves to see what areas are spasming the most. When they find the ones that are spasming they shoot the Botox into those places. It kinda hurts when they do so. I have to put my feet up on a chair as I get a little dizzy when they put it in. Putting my feet up helps anyway to diminish the spasms. I then lie down for a few minutes to regain control of my body. It takes a lot out of you. Tanya found out more problems in my left hip. I can barely rotate my hip now. I can't do basic dance steps or anything on my left leg. My whole left side is firing and spasming. They think I had my left foot really hard on the floor board of the car that all the energy went up my leg. So it constantly hurts and I can't really sit now in a comfortable position. My left hip is turned up and I am having some kind of pelvis problem. She did some kind of rotation on it and it could barely move. She also stretched it out and found some ways to give me relief.

But, I think the Botox is already starting to work as my head is a little straighter and is spasming less. All my docs including them have now given me the talk... the talk about rest. I am doing too much. It is so hard as I just so desire to be back at work, be back hanging out with friends, etc... for those of you that know me well, know that I love to be out and about... This is probably one of the hardest things I have had to deal with.

October 22, 2010-Resting was hard today. I am so not used to resting. I guess it will take some time getting used to. Sure is not fun. Spasms are strong. But I know that God is good and is going to use this for the good.

October 23, 2010-Life is so unfair. I wish I had more control over my body. I am not enjoying this season of life but I am learning to see the good in it. I know that there is good though in it. I just finished the book called Plan B. I highly recommend it. It talks about the 'plan B' of life and how we can overcome it. Sitting continues to be tough with these spasms. One of these side effects of the Botox is hoarse voice which is definitely what I am experiencing... not fun. I am so not enjoying being at home resting... I've been reading lots of books, playing lots of guitar, etc... but being a type "A" it does not help keep thinking about others things. I feel so useless not being able to do much.

Hopefully with the Botox, physical therapy, and resting that I will start to feel better soon. It is definitely a slow process, but in the mean time I am learning so much about myself and waiting. In some ways it is good to slow my life down and not be running around wild doing things. I so wish it was different, but this is where I am at in life and need to just accept it. So annoying sitting and constantly spasms start firing like crazy!

A big shout out to: my parents for watching me go through this and helping me with driving me to doctor appointments, consulting with the doctors for the best care, and for helping me with my pt work. A shout out to all my friends who have been so supportive, caring, and compassionate... thank you to everyone and thank you for your concern. This is not easy, but I thank you from the bottom of my heart for being there for me!

October 25, 2010-The positive: head is a little straighter and sleep is better

Negative: spasms continue to be intense and strong, neck hurts from being so tilted one way, and my hip is really bad still.

October 27, 2010-I had pt yesterday which was really helpful. My hip and neck seem a lot better than yesterday from what my pt worked on. There are still a lot of muscles that are spasming and firing. My nervous system is still a wreck, but I can tell things are starting to improve. It is a long slow journey. I hate waiting. Waiting in line for anything... I love Disney World, but sometimes those waits take forever. This is kinda what it feels like the waiting time. I have waiting 2 months to be healed of these spasms. Now to some of you 2 months is not a long time, but to me it is. To me having these spasms almost 24/7 with the pain it causes as well makes me feel like I am waiting for that 3 hour wait time on your favorite ride at Disney. This is definitely a plan B moment for me. I never pictured myself here at this point. Almost a year ago, I graduated from college. In doing so, I pictured myself loving life, having a full time job, continuing to pursue theatre, etc... Never pictured that I would be in pain and not able to do much, but here I am today. Realizing the fact that this has come and as many say this too shall pass. With the help from pt, I was able to finally get a full night's sleep once again, but I remain tired from the spasms and the loss of sleep that I have been getting. Don't take life for granted... you never know where you will end up. Enjoy the ride, live everyday as if it were your last, be joyful and grateful that you are alive today!

October 28, 2010-I am continued to be amazed at the ways God is working through people in my life. Remember to count your blessings and be thankful for today as tomorrow is not guaranteed. I am very blessed as yesterday a friend of mine and my mom's from her work brought over a home cooked meal to our house which was so nice of her. Thank you for touching my life! :) When will this be over? I don't know... many people have asked me if this is curable and if so how long it takes. How long? How long? I am reminded of Psalm 6 which says:

Be merciful to me, LORD, for I am faint;

O LORD, heal me, for my bones are in agony. My soul is in anguish. How long, O LORD, how long? Turn, O LORD, and deliver me; save me because of your unfailing love.

How long? The answer is I don't know. Doctors and my pt don't know... it will just take time. I have also been hearing much of God say to me which is a song: Strength will rise as we wait upon the Lord, wait upon the Lord, we will wait upon the Lord.

This summer, I had the opportunity to walk alongside a close friend go through what I am going through. I heard God sing this song to me for her. :) Now, I am hearing Him say it to me. This journey has taken such a different road than I totally expected. Today, I had pt. Man, was it painful... in a good way. :) We broke a sweet and got in a work out as my body and esp nervous system is so wrecked. My body is not able to do things it was two months ago. It will be two months ago that the spasms started tomorrow. It has been a long two months. I know that Jill is doing everything she can to help me which I am thankful for and trusting that what is she is doing is good. I know my body is changing and is slowly correcting itself to where it should be. It is a long slow process though and very painful. After pt which was 45 minutes of spasming like crazy, I rested the rest of the day... still very exhausted from it. Think about having someone try to work on you while your body is constantly spasming. Jill is having me to do this exercise with a towel and me trying to sway my left leg back and forth which in theory for most people is easy to do. I was able to do it with no problem before the accident. Now, it seems impossible to do. WOW! We are also discussing the option of possibly more Botox, not sure though if more is better or not. It is a difficult situation to know what will help. This has been the most difficult and challenging experiences probably I have ever experienced, but I know that my God is good and He is faithful to his promises. I am healed in Jesus' name. In the Twin Cities, we have everything. I am so thankful that today we have medicine like Botox, doctors like Dr. Dykstra, pts like Jill, and loving people who have supported me... :) I know that I would not have been able to go through this without all of you, your support, and words of encouragement, concern, care, love, and prayers.

October 30, 2010-Dystonia is an hour by hour thing. One hour I am doing fine and am improving and the next the spasms are going crazy. Sitting makes spasms worse. It is not something I hope anyone has to go through. Sitting just to type this is making the spasms go. My left hip is really hurting. It makes it hard to walk too.

November 1, 2010-Woke up a couple of times last night due to the spasms... but was able to sleep more this morning which was good. I really wish this would hurry up!

November 3, 2010-

The spasms were difficult today.... really pulling hard. There are good hours and bad hours of the day... I am really learning to REST, although as I said before it is a slow and challenging process. Also, I had physical therapy with both Jill. It was really good. I feel like I get relief. I feel good for a few days and then the spasms pull hard. I am praying and hoping for not only a cure, but also for an answer, a solution, wisdom of what to do, as I long to be healed. Every single time I go to physical therapy, I am dying in sweat as it is truly a workout there. It is challenging. My head is still twisted to the right and I can't get it straight... it is straightening out though slowly but surely. I am really hoping to not only be healed so that I can continue to work and live my life, but also to continue to pursue theatre. I miss being in a show!

November 6, 2010-I have not had much energy to write and be on the computer much. I have been actually been able to rest and sleep which is good. My energy is quite diminished. I can be at peace for about an hour and then have to go and rest which of course makes things difficult. I try to work and get exhausted. Going to run simple errands exhausts me. My body is so not good. Nervous system is going crazy. People say that it is like my body is on a marathon always working hard and exercising. It rarely gets a break. The spasms really never stop. This is the reason I sweat so much. I don't like not being able to work out, but this truly a workout currently. It is working out all the time. There was a point in this in which I lost weight because my body was using it all with the spasms. I continue to see improvements. There are times when I feel so encouraged and times when I want to give up...it is so painful. I hope no one gets this. This is not fun and something that I hope no one experiences. This is probably the hardest thing I've had to deal with in my wonderful 24 years of life. I know I will come out stronger from this though so Praise God! He will use this for His glory... but in the meantime, wow! It continues to truly be a journey... so much pain... There are times it is so unbearable. The spasms go crazy and there is nothing I can do for it. It pulls my head the right and my hip out/up... I know that this too shall pass, but I am having such a hard time with this. I feel so helpless, I wish I could do something about this...I wish there was a magic pill or something that I could do or take, but sadly there is not. My left one is still spasming a lot and pushing forward which makes sitting and laying down a problem. My walking has become slower because of this. It is scary to see how much movement I have lost in my left leg/hip. I can barely move it. The exercise I have to do are so simple on the right side, but with the left side it is like I'm teaching it to move again like I'm a baby teaching it to work again.

I talked with Tanya (Dr. Dykstra's) coworker on Thursday. She was so encouraging to me. She gave me some good ideas to sit, sleep, etc... I'm trying to learn as I have a new body and how it functions. It is all a game, an experiment of trying different ways and seeing which ways help make the spasms better and not start firing a lot. There are some better positions to be in that help somewhat and some that as soon as I go into them it is unbearable. As Tanya and Jill have explained to me that everyone with dystonia is so different in their patterns of movement that there is no one answer or one way to cure this and no way of knowing how long it will take. Everyone has their own different perceptive of how to handle this... more

Botox? Pain medications? More pt? What? Please pray for wisdom of the doctors and team of people working with me that we can find what is best for my body. I am not sure... It is hard to tell what will be best. I don't want to throw too much at my body but I'm not sure what is the best way to handle such an unknown thing. Everyone has their own opinion of what to do and right now there are conflicting opinions... all from experts in their fields... looks at this point that I am going to be monitored closely by Dr. Dykstra and Tanya and continuing to see Jill of course about twice a week. I am really hoping that PT starts to last longer. PT is so helpful. I am able to sleep better with having PT, yet I feel like it lasts for a day or two and then it goes back to spasming all over the place. I just want a quick fix and cure. I talked with Tanya about this. I just want to be healed, so I can resume life, as currently life is on hold. She explained it to me that I am in Life College. She has I need to rest and have patience... both of I am not good at. I am learning good valuable lessons here such as patience, waiting, resting...very hard and difficult lessons...lessons that I don't want to be. I would rather be on plan A and not plan B. I would so much rather not be in life college.... but not my will, but your be done. I am trusting that there is a purpose in this.

November 7, 2010-It has been 11 weeks since the accident... 2 months and a week or so. It sure has been a long, tiresome, warring, not fun, painful, dark, and confusing at time process. I am continuing to try to stay positive through the challenging times.

Today a song was in my head it goes like this:

Blessed be your name when I'm found in the desert place, though I walk through the wilderness, Blessed be your name.

Blessed be your name on the road marked with suffering, those their pain in the offering, blessed be your name.

I want you to think about this:

Picture yourself eating at the dinner table. Notice how easy it is for you to pick up your fork and get the food on your fork into your mouth. Easy, brainless right? Well... not for me...

Next, picture yourself trying to bring your knees to your chest to stretch your back, easy position right... well... not for me...

Picture yourself sitting in the car, by your computer, easy brainless right? well... not for me...

Picture yourself sleeping, again difficult for me.

Finally, picture yourself taking a shower... for most of you easy job right? well, again not for me...

I feel as though I am truly walking through the desert. As, this is so difficult. Simple patterns or ways of life are difficult for me. So as you do basic things around yourself... eating, sleeping, sitting, driving, showering, etc, be thankful that you can do this with no pain. Every movement, I literally have to think about. Even though, I am very blessed to have so many people around to support me and love on me, it is hard at times... many people don't understand dystonia or know much about it. I encourage you to read about it on the internet, find out it, and research this amazing condition. My heart goes out to those who have it especially due to the fact that it is not curable and hard to diagnose, cure, and treat. I am continuing to HEAL IN JESUS! I still have trouble turning my head with the spasms, so obviously makes driving difficult as well as working.

Many of you asked if I can asked if I can drive: Answer: yes and no, if it is close then I could. I try not to though. The spasms get worse when I drive and turning my head is difficult. I try to get rides from others at this point. My doc/pt/parents are concerned as well when I drive for my safety.

The medication continues to make me sleepy and a little drowsy. I used to be so type A on the go etc...

now I feel so relaxed... still with the spasms, but it is different. Kinda weird, I feel so chill that I used to be. But, man does it make me sleepy.

November 8, 2010-As always, I got beat up today in physical therapy. I am so exhausted from it. I think it is helping though. Jill worked on my hip and neck...it is all going really crazy. The exercises are so hard! I can't keep my left hip from going up. Thanks to Sheila and my dad for taking me to PT today. I really appreciate it as does Jill! I can't wait and hope to be healed soon! Although, I know that this is all part of my testimony!

MAKE THE PULLING STOP!!!!! AHHHHHHHHH-HH!!!!

November 9, 2010-Life is good... despite the pulling of neck and the uncontrollable spasms in my body, and my nervous system screwed up, and my left hip unable to do stuff, etc... I know that my God is good and has a plan a purpose for my life! Like Tanya said and others, I am in the school of trust, patience, waiting, healing, and many of schools. Very hard time, but I know that God works for the good of those that trust in Him. Strength will rise as we wait upon the Lord.

November 10, 2010-Thanks for your all your support, prayers, and love. It means so much to me during this hard, difficult, challenging time. I know that some of you have asked how you could help me.... a few things if you are in the area:

1. I have many physical therapy appointments that are hard for me to drive to. I could use rides there and back.

2. Meal-If you would like to drop off a meal to my family or me during lunch time that would be helpful.

3. Or simply taking me out to coffee, would be such a blessing to me

If you don't live close:

1. Prayers

2. Encouragement
3. Simple email

At this present time, I am unable to drive and unable to work much. I still can't turn my head, so driving is both difficult and dangerous. Also, I don't have the strength or energy to work many hours. This has got to be one the hardest things is that I can't work or drive. I have always had a car and was able to drive and now having to rely mostly on my family and others to drive me place is a real challenge. I appreciate all those who have helped me though get to places. You never know what life will throw at you, I was hoping by this time, I would be working full time as a teacher, but God gave me something different to deal with... a new challenge in life... a challenge of rest, a challenge of peace, a challenge of patience, a challenge of waiting, and much others... not the road I would have chosen if you asked me.

The spasms are strong and are pulling hard. It is so not fun. I am so trying to stay positive with the whole thing, but it is very challenging. The docs have no idea when it will be cured and I am getting so frustrated that it is not soon. It has been such a long few months for me!!!!!! HELP! The pain is so much. The c1 and c2 vertebrae are just not lining up!!!! I feel so helpless at times.

I am also taking a new medication as a muscle relaxant due to conditions of my heart, I am only allowed to take a very small dosage. I've only been on it for a few days, so we are still testing it to see if it will work. I'm not 100% sure how much it is helping. I know that I am able to get more sleep however. It does put me to sleep. After taking it I get so tired! It makes me very sleepy/drowsy.

Since there is also no cure for dystonia it is all a game. Every person with dystonia is so different in their movements and patterns. For me it is my neck spasmsing to the right making my head not straight.

Also it has affected my whole nervous system which is firing and especially my left hip. It is quite scary how much movement mobility I have lost in that side of my body. It kinda hurts to walk. My physical therapist is having me do exercises (which are really easy for most and were for me before the accident) and now on the left side it is scary to see all that movement being lost. I really want to be able to dance again in doing a show, but we will see. Doctors can do Botox injections (which I have gotten some, might be getting more sometime before Christmas), physical therapy, and medication. The medication, however, is only a Band-Aid for the problem and doesn't "cure" anything. I really wish there was a cure for dystonia. They just haven't found anything yet which is the discouraging thing. So it is all a game, an experiment, to see what works and what doesn't for my body. Sitting hurts, showering hurts, laying down sometimes hurts....as many who see me say in a good way...I'm a mess!

It is all a matter of time! It is such a different life-style though...being a type A, always busy, always on the go, always doing something.... (all in good ways) this has caused me to slow down. The medicine has helped. It has calmed me down a lot and relaxed me. My body is so jazzed up right now. It is like taking ADD medication and it changes your body and it changes you!

To read the rest of Nikki's journal entries, visit:
www.caringbridge.org/nikkiabramson

Journal Discussion Questions

Use these pages to journal your stories, your ideas, your visions, and your life journey. These questions are here to guide you. I am here for you. I'd love to hear your thoughts. Please feel free to contact me.

1. What are some areas that you need to overcome? How can you overcome them?
2. Are you adopted? Do you know someone who is adopted? What are your thoughts on adoption?
3. How have you seen your life change?
4. How did your view of adoption and cultural identity differ or change based on Nikki's story?
5. Do you battle a disability or a physical ailment? Know someone who does? How did your view of people with disabilities differ or change based on Nikki's story? How does this change your view on disabilities?
6. Do you have mentors in your life? If so, how have they helped develop you? Are you mentoring anyone? Are you challenging them?
7. What does it mean to have hope? How can you take Nikki's acronym of hope and apply it to your life?
8. If there are one or two words or phrases you want to live by, what are they?
9. Are you a positive person? Do you tend to see the glass half empty or half full? How do you stay positive?
10. What can you do to fill your emotional, spiritual, and physical tank?
11. Which of the "food for thoughts" has evoked something in you that spurs you on to more?
12. Are you taking life for granted? What can you start doing now to appreciate every minute?
13. What can you do to help others have hope?
14. What inspires you?

Everyone has a story. Even you! What is your story? You may not be a writer—I didn't consider myself a writer for a long time—but share your story with others. We need to hear each other's stories.

Journal Pages

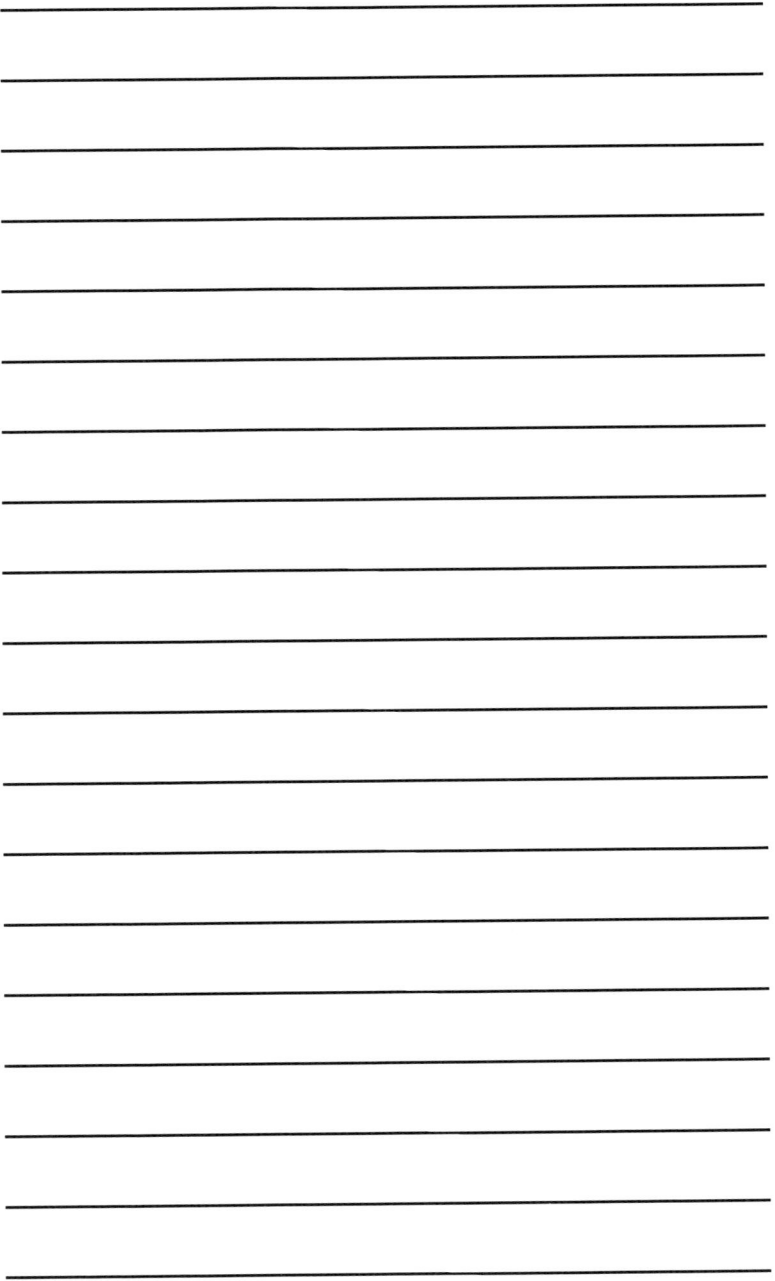

Nikki Min Yeong Abramson

I Choose Hope

Overcoming Challenges with Faith and Positivity

Resources:

This is a compilation of resources that have influenced me in my quest to choose hope. I hope you find it helpful to you as much as it has been for me.

Adoption Groups:
AK Connection
AdopSource
Children's Home Society
Korean Quarterly
Land of Gazillion Adoptees
Lutheran Social Services
MN Adopt
Resource Committee Adopted Adults (RCAA)

Books:
7 Habits of Highly Effective People by Stephen Covey
Bible (NIV translation)
Beyond Me by Melinda Doolittle
Courage to Teach by Parker Palmer
Crazy Love by Francis Chan
Divine Mentor by Wayne Cordeiro
Escape Adulthood by Jason Kotecki
Fish by Stephen Lundin
Our Town by Thorton Wilder
Purpose Driven Life by Rick Warren
Soul Surfer by Bethany Hamiliton
Surrender to Love by David Benner
The Filter by Jeff Londraville
The Me I Want To Be by John Ortberg
Wild Goose Chase by Mark Batterson

Churches:
Christ Presbyterian Church
Upper Room Community
Wooddale Church

Medical Care Facilitates:
Abbot/Allina Health Systems
Gillette Children's/Lifetime Clinics
Health Partners Clinics
University of Minnesota Med School

Movies:
Cool Runnings
Hairspray
Karate Kid
Mamma Mia
Mighty Ducks 2 and 3
Remember the Titans
Soul Surfer
Sister Act 1 and 2
What a Girl Wants
Wizard of Oz

Music:
Beauty from Pain by Superchick
Blessings by Laura Story
Calling All Angels by Train
Dare You to Move by Switchfoot
Don't Stop Believing by Journey
Fix You by Coldplay
He's Always Been Faithful by Sara Goves
Hope Take Hold by Stefan Van Voorst
I Have a Dream by ABBA
I Won't Give Up by Jason Mraz
Live Like You're Dying by Kris Allen
Only Hope by Mandy Moore
So Small by Carrie Underwood
Stronger by Kelly Clarkson
Temporary Home by Carrie Underwood
What Faith Can Do by Kutless
When You Believe by Whitney Houston
You Raise Me Up by Josh Groban/Secret Garden
You Can't Stop the Beat by Hairspray

Musicals:
Joseph and the Amazing Technicolor Dreamcoat
Wicked the Musical

Organizations:
Caring Bridge Company
DMRF (Dystonia Medical Foundation)
Disney World
MDA (Musuclar Dystrophy Association)
ST Dystonia

Schools:
Bethel University
International School of Minnesota

Follow Nikki Min Yeong Abramson

I would love to hear from you. Please follow my blogs via my websites and social networking sites.

Personal website: www.nikkiabramson.com
Renew Hope, LLC: www.renewingyourhope.com
For comments, questions, and feedback, please email Nikki at: nikki@nikkiabramson.com
For bookings and inquires for speaking, please email Ms. Abramson at: nikki@renewingyourhope.com

Social Networking Sites:

Facebook: /nikkiabramson
Twitter: @NikAbramson
Linked In: nikkiabramson
Youtube Channel: nikabramson

Rivershore Books: www.rivershorebooks.com
Jansina: Jansina@rivershorebooks.com

About the Author

Nikki Abramson is passionate about encouraging people through their life journeys. She is a Korean American adoptee who battles several rare and severe medical conditions and is overcoming many obstacles. Nikki resides in Minneapolis, Minnesota. She lives with her parents, younger brother, and two cats. Nikki is a proud alum of International School of MN (Eden Prairie, MN) 2005 and Bethel University (St. Paul, MN) 2009. She holds a B.A. and teaching license in elementary education, early childhood, and computers, keyboarding, and technology. Ms. Abramson is a performer and teaching artist, teaching others acting, improv, and choreographing. She also has a company, Renew Hope, LLC, that consists of motivational speaking and life coaching. Her desire in life is to change the world by inspiring others through her story, changing one person at a time. Nikki is an advocate for those that are overcoming challenges and is involved with adoption communities and people with disabilities communities as well. In Nikki's spare time, she enjoys Caribou coffee dates, Mexican food, musical theatre, playing board games, music, scrapbooking, Disney World, and spending time with friends and family.

For more information, you may contact her via her websites at www.nikkiabramson.com or www.renewingyourhope.com.

Jansina: Owner and Editor, Rivershore Books
www.rivershorebooks.com

Jansina is an editor and an author and can't remember a time she didn't love words. In 2012, she began her editing and publishing company, Rivershore Books. The business began out of a desire to help her fellow authors see their books in print while doing something she enjoyed, and it is continuing to grow. Her goal is to honor God in her writing and encourage others to do the same.

Kiera Johnson: Photographer

Kiera Johnson is a freelance photographer and cinematographer and is currently a film student at Emerson College in Boston. Kiera attended high school at the International School of Minnesota in Eden Prairie, Minnesota and resides in Minnesota when not in school. She enjoys bright colors, writing, house music, warm air, and large amounts of wind and water. Feel free to check out her website at www.colorhill. com.

Katherine Pjevach: Illustrator

Katherine is a sophomore at Washington University in St. Louis who is studying Biology and Pre-Veterinary Studies. In her spare time, she enjoys being in the outdoors and spending time with her dog, Dixie. In addition, she loves to do anything related to art. Her favorite medium is watercolor, and she loves to paint landscapes. She intends to continue with art along with her studies in the ensuing years.

Amber Walker: Hair and Makeup Artist

Amber Walker is a professional hair and makeup artist. She has been working with Nikki over the past ten years.
www.awhairandmakeup.com or
www.onsitemuse.com

Scott Werley: Creative Professional and Cover Designer

A young, extroverted entrepreneur of 26 years, Scott originally hails from Minneapolis, Minnesota and is currently residing in the tech-driven San Francisco Bay Area. He is the Creative Director of Scott Werley Creative and has recently accepted a full time lead design position with Razorfrog Web Design in the heart of the city. Scott is a devoted web and graphic design professional. When not designing logos and WordPress websites for thriving small businesses, he spends his time exploring nature, visiting wine country with his wife Lindsey, cooking tasty dishes, and spoiling his cat named "J. Charles." www.scottwerleycreative.com www.linkedin.com/in/scottwerley

Dani Werner: Author Headshot Photographer
www.daniphoto.com

Dani has enjoyed a wonderful career as a professional portrait photographer for over fifteen years. She states that it has been a privilege to work with such a diverse range of interesting and talented people. Every day brings new opportunities and inspiration.

Inspirational | Memoir | Self-Improvement

Being told by doctors at the age of five that she would die in her teens, Nikki Abramson learned how to live in the present. Mentors taught her how to overcome challenges and obstacles through faith and believing in the power of positivity. Nikki addresses what it is like to want to 'fit in' with society through her struggles as an international adoptee and battling serious rare disabilities. Her courage to go on when life is challenging is an inspiration to all. Nikki spells out what hope means to her. Finding hope is not easy and is an everyday battle. "Struggles are a part of life. We can either go through it with a cloud over our head, or we can look at it as an opportunity." She sees life as an opportunity: to help others discover their potential and to make a difference in their lives. This book includes pictures of Nikki's life, beautiful illustrations, and journal and discussion questions to reflect upon one's own life experiences.

"*I Choose Hope* is an inspiring memoir of one Korean adoptee's life journey of hope, faith, and perseverance through adversity, shattered dreams, and racial identity. This book offers a raw look into the life of a person who has experienced many challenges, but who has found hope, healing, and joy despite pain and disappointments. Readers will be amazed at [Nikki's] inner strength, determination, and unbreakable spirit..."

– *Sarah Easton, Adoption Social Worker*

"Regardless of the many challenges she has been dealt in her life, Ms. Abramson has managed to maintain a positive perspective and now uses her story to motivate others. Her journey through adoption and a complex cultural identity, in conjunction with several medical conditions, are important reminders of our ability to persevere in the face of adversity."

– *Jack Pipkin, Executive Director, Muscular Dystrophy Association*

"It has been quite some time since I picked up a book and got so riveted by it that I could not put it down. Nikki has an indomitable spirit that serves as a beacon of hope to all... If you are looking for a book that teaches you how to keep moving forward – how to make "hope" the single focus of your life – look no more; this book is for you."

– *Roger Soweid, SABIS® Corporate Director, Student Life and Student Management*

For more about Nikki visit:
renewingyourhope.com
nikkiabramson.com

Copyright © 2014 Nikki Abramson,
Renew Hope LLC. All Rights Reserved.
Published by Rivershore Books.
www.rivershorebooks.com

Made in the USA
San Bernardino, CA
01 March 2014